*The Way of
the Guerrilla*

The Way of the Guerrilla

Achieving Success and Balance as an Entrepreneur in the 21st Century

JAY CONRAD LEVINSON

HOUGHTON MIFFLIN COMPANY

Boston New York 1997

For information about permission to reproduce selections from
this book, write to Permissions, Houghton Mifflin Company,
215 Park Avenue South, New York, New York 10003.

For information about this and other Houghton Mifflin
trade and reference books and multimedia products, visit
The Bookstore at Houghton Mifflin on the World Wide Web
at http://www.hmco.com/trade/.

Library of Congress Cataloging-in-Publication Data
Levinson, Jay Conrad.
   The way of the Guerrilla : achieving success and balance as
an entrepreneur in the 21st century / Jay Conrad Levinson.
      p.   cm.
   ISBN 0-395-77018-1
   1. Entrepreneurship.   I. Title.
   HB615.L48   1997
   658.4'21 — dc20   96-34958   CIP

Printed in the United States of America

QUM 10 9 8 7 6 5 4 3 2 1

It's a joy to dedicate this book to
Norm Goldring and Vicki Gross,
who know the way

Contents

Introduction

ALL ABOARD! You're about to leave one century and enter another, whether you like it or not. That means leaving behind many things you've grown to know and love—or hate. And it means embracing new ways of thinking, new ways of working, new ways of living. Open wide the doors of change, and opportunities will come rushing through.

To entrepreneurs, the changes will be dramatic. They'll be moving from an age characterized by a worship of profits, a surfeit of working hours, and a neglect of family and self—to a new age in which twentieth-century business practices will no longer be workable and the path to follow will be the way of the guerrilla.

The way of the guerrilla will still lead toward profits, but not at the expense of draconian working hours or the sacrificing of time with your family, time for yourself. The twentieth-century entrepreneur was a risk-taker who paid a high price for success—if, indeed, financial success ever came. The twenty-first-century entrepreneur will also be a risk-taker, but will be more assured of success. He will define that success by not only the standard notion of finances, but also the blessed notion of balance—between work and leisure, between work and family, between work and humanity, between work and self. The twenty-first-century entrepreneur will be a guerrilla entrepreneur, for only the guerrilla entrepreneur seeks and finds success beyond the profit-and-loss statement, beyond the workplace.

Today, there are more entrepreneurs than ever, but few true guerrilla entrepreneurs. If you are contemplating the life of an entrepreneur, the way of the guerrilla is the path you should follow. If you are already an entrepreneur, that is the direction in which you should evolve.

Guerrilla entrepreneurship did not exist for your parents or for your grandparents, because the path has only recently been blazed. Technology and enlightenment have marked its way. The Puritan work ethic of your ancestors has gone by the wayside, along with the Puritans. That work ethic had no place for balance, only for hard work. The guerrilla work ethic includes both.

Blending the cream of the twentieth century into the elixir of the twenty-first, the way of the guerrilla will not require that you leave every one of your business practices behind, only the things that I've discovered won't work for you. It will not ask that you become involved in everything new, only the things likely to work for you. The hallmarks of the guerrilla's trail are the best of the old ways (sane working hours, time for your family, humane treatment of employees) and the best of the new ways (time-saving technology, advanced communication techniques, enlightened attitudes toward work).

The benefits of the guerrilla's way range from individual to global in scope. They reveal undiscovered opportunities as plentiful and sparkling as raindrops in spring. They ask not that you aim high, but that you aim sensibly. They allow you to reach your goals sooner than you may have expected.

The way of the guerrilla makes profits the third priority, well ahead of sales and leads, but well behind humanity and balance. To embark upon this way, you'll first need the right goals, and then you'll need the proper setting. Once these are in place, you'll require the tools for success. And finally, you'll need the secret tricks of the trade to sustain you. All are contained in this book. All are yours for the taking.

PART I

The Goals

Welcome to the close of one millennium and the dawn of a radiant, promising new one. And congratulations on even considering becoming a guerrilla entrepreneur in a new, rapidly changing world. It's challenging, but you're in for a lot of fun. Work? Of course, lots of work. But fun, too. Lots of fun, if you do it right. And this is the first page of how to do it right.

The first thing you'll notice about being a guerrilla entrepreneur is that your goals will be different from the old-fashioned goals of a nonguerrilla entrepreneur. A guerrilla enterprise is flexible, innovative, unconventional, low in overhead costs, dependent, interactive, generous, enjoyable, and profitable. The goal of the enterprise is to stay that way.

Look at the entrepreneurs all around you. If you can't see many, it's because they are not guerrillas; instead, they're buried in work, rarely coming up for the fresh air of free time. The goals of guerrilla entrepreneurs allow them the freedom to pursue interests beyond work—while amassing an income beyond that of their workaholic ancestors.

You can always tell guerrilla entrepreneurs by their goals. They are not as money-minded as the entrepreneurs who came before them. They seem to be happier with the work that they're doing and appear to care like crazy about satisfying the needs of their customers. You've never seen follow-up done the way these people do it. They stay in touch *constantly* with their customers. It's not as if they are working at their business, but rather demonstrating *passion* for their work. Their goal is to express that passion with excellence and transform it into profits.

Not surprisingly, guerrilla entrepreneurs achieve their goals on a daily basis. Their long-term goals are lofty. Those goals exist in the future. Their short-term goals are even more lofty. Those exist in the *present*—for that is the domain of the guerrilla. That is where her goals are to be found in abundance.

Your ability to plan for the future and learn from the past will determine your level of comfort in the present, in the here and now. Being a guerrilla entrepreneur means realizing that these can be the good old days and that you don't have to wait for the joy that comes with success. It's there in front of you, frolicking in the upcoming pages.

1

The New American Dream

WAKE UP from the Old American Dream, and realize that it has changed for the better—it is more achievable, more enjoyable, and much healthier than the old one.

Although at this moment you may find the New American Dream unconventional—as are all guerrilla endeavors—you'll soon see that it will come to be the mainstream American Dream, because it is achievable and brings increased benefits. Most of us can dream it and then delight in making it come true.

Originally, the dream meant having enough food and protection from the weather. Cave dwellers dreamt of hunting enough game or gathering an abundance of nuts and berries. That dream changed, replaced by the hope of earning enough money to feed a hungry family. The Industrial Revolution took care of that and eventually gave birth to the American Dream: a house, a job, and financial security.

The oldest American Dream

Entrepreneurs of the twentieth century were motivated by a slightly different version of the American Dream. In place of a house, a job, and financial security, they sought fortune, security, expansion, and power. But that journey was characterized by workaholism, sacrifice, and greed.

The entrepreneur of the twenty-first century will be more of a guerrilla—one who thrives on the nontraditional, does the unconventional if the conventional is nonsensical, and knows that working in the new millennium requires rethinking the nature of being a successful entrepreneur.

Entrepreneurs in the twenty-first century will be motivated by the *journey itself*, for the journey will be the goal.

Balance will be the new dream. Guerrilla entrepreneurs who go about creating a profit-producing enterprise will begin with balance, actually *starting* with work that makes them happy, the goal of all guerrilla dreams. Once that has been attained, guerrilla entrepreneurs will be able to pursue their other goals: making money, enjoying free time, maintaining health, and having fun.

When the journey is the goal, you can begin with work that satisfies you, time to spend enjoying activities other than the work you love, and a remarkable freedom from work-related stress. Guerrilla entrepreneurs, many of whom exist today, well ahead of their time, have twenty characteristics in common. These twenty hallmarks fuel the commitment these entrepreneurs have—to themselves, their families, their communities, and their work.

The journey is the goal

1. *The guerrilla entrepreneur knows that the journey is the goal.* He also realizes that he is in control of his enterprise, not the other way around, and that if he is dissatisfied with his journey, he is missing the point of the journey itself. Unlike old-fashioned enterprises, which often required gigantic sacrifices for the sake of the goal, guerrilla enterprises place the goal of a pleasant journey ahead of the mere notion of sacrifices.

2. *The guerrilla entrepreneur achieves balance from the very start.* She builds free time into her work schedule so that balance is part of her enterprise. She respects her leisure time as much as her work time, never allowing too much of one to interfere with the other. Traditional entrepreneurs always placed work ahead of leisure and showed no respect for their own personal freedom. Guerrillas cherish their freedom as much as their work.

3. *The guerrilla entrepreneur is not in a hurry.* Unnecessary speed frequently undermines even the best-conceived strategies. Haste makes waste and sacrifices quality. The guerrilla is fully aware that patience is his ally, and he has planned intelligently

to eliminate most emergencies that call for moving fast. His pace is always steady but never rushed.

4. *The guerrilla entrepreneur uses stress as a benchmark.* If she feels any stress, she knows she must be going about things in the wrong way. Guerrilla entrepreneurs do not accept stress as part of doing business and recognize any stress as a warning sign that something's the matter—in the work plan of the guerrilla or in the business itself. Adjustments are made to eliminate the *cause* of the stress, which causes the stress to disappear.

A warning sign

5. *The guerrilla entrepreneur looks forward to work.* He has a love affair with his work and considers himself blessed to be paid for doing the work he does. He is good at his work, energizing his passion for it in a quest to learn more about it and improve his understanding of it, thereby increasing his skills. The guerrilla entrepreneur doesn't think about retirement, for he would never want to stop doing the work he loves.

6. *The guerrilla entrepreneur has no weaknesses.* She is effective in every aspect of her enterprise because she has filled in the gaps between her strengths and talents with people who abound in the prowess she lacks. She is very much a team player and allies herself with other guerrillas who share the team spirit and possess complementary skills. She values her teammates as much as old-fashioned entrepreneurs valued their independence.

7. *The guerrilla entrepreneur is fusion-oriented.* He is always on the alert to fuse his business with other synergistic enterprises in town, in America, in the world. He is willing to combine marketing efforts, production skills, information, leads, mailing lists, and anything else to increase his effectiveness and marketing reach while reducing the cost of achieving those goals. His fusion efforts are intentionally short-term and rarely permanent. In his business relationships, instead of thinking "marriage," he thinks "fling."

8. *The guerrilla entrepreneur does not kid herself.* She knows that if she overestimates her own abilities, she runs the risk of skimping on the quality she represents to her customers, em-

No kidding

ployees, investors, suppliers, and fusion partners. She forces herself to face reality on a daily basis and realizes that all of her business practices must always be evaluated in the glaring light of
what is really happening, instead of what should be happening.

9. *The guerrilla entrepreneur lives in the present.* He is well
aware of the past, very enticed by the future, but the here and
now is where he resides, embracing the technologies of the
present, leaving future technologies on the horizon right where
they belong—until later, when they are ripe and ready. He is
alert to the new, wary of the avant-garde, and wooed from the old
only by improvement, not mere change.

10. *The guerrilla entrepreneur understands the precious nature of time.* She doesn't buy into the old lie that time is money
and knows in her heart that time is far more important than
money. She knows that time is *life.* She is aware that her customers and prospects feel the same way about time, so she respects
theirs and wouldn't dare waste it. As a practicing guerrilla, she is
the epitome of efficiency but never lets it interfere with her
effectiveness.

11. *The guerrilla entrepreneur always operates according to a
plan.* He knows who he is, where he is going, and how he will
get there. He is prepared, knows that anything can and will
happen, and can deal with the barriers to entrepreneurial success because his plan has foreseen them and shown exactly how
to surmount them. The guerrilla reevaluates his plan regularly
and does not hesitate to make changes in it, though commitment to the plan is part of his very being.

12. *The guerrilla entrepreneur is flexible.* She is guided by a
strategy for success and knows the difference between a guide
and a master. When it is necessary, the guerrilla changes, accepting change as part of the status quo, not ignoring or battling
it. She is able to adapt to new situations, realizes that service is
whatever her customers want it to be, and knows that inflexible
things become brittle and break.

*A guide,
not a master*

13. *The guerrilla aims for results more than growth.* He is
focused on profitability and balance, vitality and improvement,
value and quality, more than size and growth. His plan calls for

steadily increasing profits without a sacrifice of personal time, so his actions are oriented to hitting those targets instead of growing for the sake of growth alone. He is wary of becoming large and does not equate hugeness with excellence.

14. *The guerrilla entrepreneur is dependent upon many people.* She knows that the age of the lone wolf entrepreneur, independent and proud of it, has passed. The guerrilla is very dependent upon her fusion business partners, her employees, her customers, her suppliers, and her mentors. She got where she is with her own wings, her own determination, her own smarts, and, as a guerrilla, with a little help from a lot of friends.

A little help from her friends

15. *The guerrilla entrepreneur is constantly learning.* A sea gull flies in circles in the sky, looking for food in an endless quest. When it finally finds the food, the sea gull lands and eats its fill. When it has completed the meal, it returns to the sky, only to fly in circles again, searching for food although it has eaten. Humans have only one comparable instinct: the need for constant learning. Guerrilla entrepreneurs have this need in spades.

16. *The guerrilla entrepreneur is passionate about work.* Her enthusiasm for what she does is apparent to everyone who sees her work. This enthusiasm spreads to everyone who works with her, even to her customers. In its purest form, this enthusiasm is best expressed as the word *passion*—an intense feeling that burns within her and is manifested in the devotion she demonstrates toward her business.

17. *The guerrilla entrepreneur is focused on the goal.* He knows that balance does not come easily and that he must rid himself of the values and expectations of his ancestors. To do this, he must remain focused on his journey, seeing the future clearly while concentrating on the present. He is aware that the minutiae of life and business can distract him, so he does what is necessary to make those distractions only momentary.

18. *The guerrilla entrepreneur is disciplined about the tasks at hand.* She is keenly aware that every time she writes a task on her daily calendar, she is making a promise to herself. As a guerrilla who does not kid herself, she keeps those promises, knowing that

the achievement of her goals will be more than an adequate reward for her discipline. She finds it easy to be disciplined because of the payback offered by the leisure that follows.

19. *The guerrilla entrepreneur is well organized at home and at work.* He does not waste valuable time looking for items that have been misplaced and stays organized as he works and as new work comes to him. His astute sense of order is fueled by the efficiency that results from it, and he shares his ability to organize with those who work with him. Yet the guerrilla never squanders precious time by becoming overorganized.

20. *The guerrilla entrepreneur has an upbeat attitude.* Because she knows that life is unfair, that problems arise, that to err is human, and that the cool shall inherit the earth, she manages to take obstacles in stride, keeping her perspective and her sense of humor. Her ever-present optimism is grounded in an ability to perceive the positive side of things—recognizing the negative, but never dwelling on it. Her positive attitude is contagious and spreads rapidly.

Life as a fairy tale

Perhaps in light of these twenty criteria, you're thinking, "Do guerrilla entrepreneurs exist in real life or only in fairy tales?" The answer is yes, they do exist in real life, but their success and balance are like a fairy tale. They exist all around you, in every state of the Union, in every nation on earth, in every ethnic minority, in all age groups, in both genders.

Armed with the right vision and the right information, guerrilla entrepreneurs can attain heights never envisioned by their parents. They can add the element of love to their work, for they will devote themselves only to work that they love.

Kahlil Gibran, in *The Prophet*, said that "work is love made visible. And if you cannot work with love but only with distaste, it is better that you should leave your work and sit at the gate of the temple and take alms of those who work with joy." Spoken like a true guerrilla.

This book has been written to make the dream vividly clear to you. For if you can see the dream, you can will it to come true.

And if you can will it to come true, you can take the steps to empower your will with actions.

Guerrillas do more than read books and attend seminars about achievement and success. They take action, do something, shake the tree. They know that their time on earth is limited, that the most important time is *right now*, and that they've got to get it right the first time. To do this, they go with the flow—*their own flow*—possessing the sensitivity to know what they really want, what they can do well, what they love to do, what is realistic, and what is possible.

The guerrilla entrepreneur is a master of the *art of the possible*.

The art of the possible

What I write in these pages is all possible, for I have lived it. I didn't have the benefit of a book to plant these ideas in my head, but made them up as I went along, or realized them as I looked back. The truth is, I wouldn't have dreamt it was possible to work as I have worked, to live as I have lived. Nobody ever told me that a three-day workweek was possible. But it didn't take me long to figure it out once I moved to an area where the enticements of nature overpowered the enticements of capitalism. What's more, I discovered that nature and capitalism are quite compatible.

It won't take you long to recognize that you have all the makings of a guerrilla entrepreneur, that you can do what I am writing about, that you can live your dream, that you can work with joy, and that it won't take a bundle to get you started—or even a lot of time.

You? Living the American Dream? No. You—living the *New* American Dream.

2

The Goals of the 21st Century

THE GOALS of the twentieth-century entrepreneur were simple: securing a job, a family, a home. The goals of the twenty-first-century guerrilla entrepreneur will be considerably loftier than those of the past: attaining work that is satisfying, enough money to enjoy freedom from worry about it, health good enough to take for granted, a family or bonding with others in which you can give and receive love and support, fun that does not have to be pursued but exists in daily living, and the longevity to appreciate with wisdom that which you and those you love have achieved.

Most important, as I hope you realize, the goal of the guerrilla is the journey itself.

Guerrilla entrepreneurs set their sights on attaining these goals—as they live their dream of enjoying life in the attainment of them. But this has not been the way with most twentieth-century entrepreneurs.

Simply observing the economy, unemployment statistics, the plight of the homeless, the low level of job satisfaction among the employed—along with their secret nightmare of being laid off during a massive downsizing—vividly proves that our society isn't living up to its potential as a successful civilization.

At least ten reasons explain this situation. We've been led down ten garden paths that lead to the economic and social swamp in which we find ourselves mired at the moment. The *Ten U-turns* time has come for us to make ten U-turns. Forget what the signs say—and what your parents and teachers said about these supposedly one-way streets. U-turns are highly recommended for any traveler who wants to reach the destination, not to mention thoroughly enjoy the journey, guerrilla-style.

Ten Dirty Lies You Have Known and Loved

Are these the only ten dirty lies that stand between you and your dream? Get serious. There are many more. But these constitute a good start, and if you cease believing them, you'll be well on your way to dreamland. Amending your beliefs begins with recognizing the myths you subscribe to. Once you do that, I doubt that you'll need me to puncture the myths for you. No doubt you'll see the bright light illuminating the truth. Here are the lies that you must *stop believing:*

1. *Time is money.* This is a blatant untruth, made up by those who are on hourly wages, frequently minimum wage. Time is far more valuable than money. If you run out of money, there are many ways to get more. If you run out of time, you can't get more.

2. *Owning a business means workaholism.* People who are workaholics prefer work to every other activity, including spending time with friends, family, and interests beyond work. Workaholism is the direct result of poor planning. Owning a business should not mean that a business owns you.

The result of poor planning

3. *Marketing is expensive.* Actually, bad marketing is expensive, and good marketing is inexpensive. Guerrilla entrepreneurs wouldn't think of using expensive marketing, but they know they must get the word out about their businesses. So they utilize inexpensive marketing with skill and fervor, using time, energy, and imagination instead of the brute force of megabucks.

4. *Big corporations are like wombs.* Big corporations used to be like wombs, but these days, many are like tombs. They employ the living dead, who work with devotion yet will be squeezed out, kicking and screaming, because of merging, downsizing, cost cutting, restructuring, and bankruptcy. If you want a corporation that functions like a womb, form it yourself.

Wombs and tombs

5. *Youth is better than age.* People who believe this one are usually young. Getting old means trading in some abilities to acquire others. It means losing some body power but gaining mind power, and not making the same mistake twice, or even once. It also helps you understand yourself and realize what wisdom really is.

6. *You need a job.* You need work, no doubt about it. And a job, structured by someone other than yourself, is one form of work. But the truth for most people is that you do *not* need a standard nine-to-five job working for someone other than your-self—and if you do, expect to pay a high price: abdicating your freedom and the discovery of your unique essence. But you do need work, and work should help you enjoy your freedom and discover your essential talents. Guerrillas love their work, but they're usually jobless. They establish the structure of their work, rather than rely on an employer.

7. *Heaven is in the afterlife.* Heaven is here and heaven is now, if you know where to look for it. Living your life as though heaven existed somewhere else and in some other time means missing the point of your life. Instead, live this life so that the heaven that follows has a lot to live up to.

Learning to love learning

8. *The purpose of education is to teach facts.* The real pur-pose of education is to teach people to love learning. The more you love learning, the better informed you'll be throughout your life. Constant learning will always be your ally. Guerrillas real-ize that times are always changing and that growing up is a process that never should end.

9. *Retirement is a good thing.* Pay close attention here: retire-ment can be fatal. It often leads to inactivity, which can lead to an early demise. If you desire longevity, don't consider total retirement. People who completely retire shut down vital sys-tems in their hearts, minds, souls, and spirits. It's okay to cut down on your workload, even cut down drastically. But never eliminate it. Don't forget that the way of the guerrilla is charac-terized by balance, and retirement can lead to imbalance, not to mention boredom.

10. *If you want it done right, do it yourself.* This is the battle cry of the terminal workaholic. The battle cry of the guerrilla is "Don't do anything you can properly delegate." It is usually unwise to think nobody can do things right except you. Such a mindset means you lack the ability to train or to link with others, mandatory skills in the twenty-first century.

Once you're free of the shackles of these ten lies, you can focus on your goals, one key to succeeding as a guerrilla entrepreneur. To reach your goals, you must not only be aware of them, but also acknowledge that goals change. When I was twenty-one years old, I established my lifetime ambition: vice presidency of an advertising agency, corner office, $50,000 a year. By the time I was thirty-three, I had achieved those goals. So was that it for me?

Heck, no. What did I know about goals as a twenty-one-year-old? I knew what twenty-one-year-olds know. I didn't know about three-day weeks, San Francisco, life without a job, the paltriness of my salary in an inflationary economy. So I adjusted my goals to the times, especially to my own time. If I hadn't changed my goals, I'd still be freezing my ears off in Chicago, walking from the parking lot to my corner office. It's crucial to have goals, but also necessary to change them when appropriate—and it might be appropriate in time.

While striving for your goals, you will form a friendship with an ugly ally, one you will try to avoid. But as an entrepreneur who takes risks, you will not be unable to avoid it forever. This ally is called *failure*. Get to know it—for if you take pains to eliminate it entirely, you will live a boring life indeed. *An ugly ally*

Failure is part of the deal when you're a guerrilla entrepreneur. I have failed so many times, failure grins in recognition when it sees me. I have failed in the smoked salmon business, the exercise equipment business, the mail-order waterbed business, the personalized gift business, and—do I have to go on?—it hurts to chronicle my disasters. Just because failure is instructive and has a lesson tucked neatly into it doesn't mean it's any fun. But guerrillas learn to construct safety nets in the form of alternative sources of income, so failure isn't the ogre it used to be.

The way of the guerrilla generates several streams of income to support the guerrilla's life. If one stream dries up, financial nourishment comes from another stream. No single stream may produce enough income, but together, they create a mighty river. This enables the guerrilla entrepreneur to tap several of his abilities. Guerrillas in the coming century will not have a single career as Grandpa did. *In Search of Excellence* author Tom Peters says, "I believe, along with British management guru Charles Handy, that a 'career' tomorrow will most likely consist of a dozen jobs, on and off payrolls of large and small firms in two or three industries."

Dixie Darr, editor of "The Accidental Entrepreneur," a newsletter devoted to "self-employment for corporate refugees," adds this note: "Most of us, whether we like it or not, face a future of self-managed portfolio careers, including a variety of part-time, temporary, or seasonal work combined with work as independent contractors, consultants, and small business own-

Composite careers

ers." She describes this as having a "composite career"—a good description of a guerrilla's situation in the coming century.

As I write, over 7 million people—about 6 percent of the work force—hold more than one job. Usually the second job is not typical wage-earning employment but an alternative source of income, accomplished part-time during evenings and weekends; it is increasingly a self-owned business. Many a corporate employee has started a part-time business as a fallback in case of future layoffs. In many cases that fallback business has become a move-forward business that proves to the employee that he or she has wings and can fly alone.

Darr tells us more about a composite career: "It is more fun. It uses more of your skills and talents than any single job could, and forces you to keep developing new abilities, exploring new opportunities. Each facet of a composite career feeds the others. This is the new self-employment." It is also the way of the guerrilla entrepreneur.

The guerrilla entrepreneur is never like the sleeping man in the cartoon "Bizarro" by Dan Piraro. A miniature version of the sleeping man, who has climbed from a rope ladder within the sleeping man's head, whispers into the sleeper's ear,

> You will wake up in the morning, shave, shower, and go to work. You will perform your job adequately and endure in silence. If your mind should wander to greener pastures, you will convince yourself that there will be plenty of time for pleasure later in life. You will return home at the end of the day content to repeat the process tomorrow. As always, you will remember nothing of this visit.

The caption on the cartoon: "Why we do it."   *"Why we do it"*

Not me. Not you. Not the guerrilla entrepreneur.

That's because the guerrilla entrepreneur has tried working from home and finds that she loves it. She's got company. *Home Office Computing* magazine reports that 85 percent of those who work at home feel more relaxed (score one point for the goal of longevity); 40 percent enjoy a healthier diet (score one more point for the same goal); 39 percent take more time off (so much for the fable about self-employed people having to work longer and harder); 32 percent feel that they have a better marriage (I'd give this point to the goals of bonding and fun); 98 percent are happier in general (one more point for fun); 96 percent recommend working at home (the other 4 percent must have a houseful of kids); and 88 percent say they'll never again return to the corporate world (one point for each of the guerrilla goals).

Does it seem as though I am asking you to break the rules in order to become a flourishing entrepreneur? Well, yes. You've got it right. Tom Peters, this time in his book *Liberation Management,* points out that the United States was shaped by rulebreakers—Ben Franklin, Tom Paine, Thomas Jefferson, Abraham Lincoln, Andrew Carnegie, Henry Ford, John D. Rockefeller, J. P. Morgan—and you? I sure hope so.

Bill Gates, the billion-dollar guerrilla who cofounded Microsoft and is a pretty successful rule-breaker himself, says of

Living for the long term

starting your own company, "The things you know and love and see opportunities in—you ought to pick your business based on that." Sure, sure, sure, you can make a pile of money doing something for the short term, but the problem is the long term. You're not living life for the short term. If you were, you'd get burned out and stressed out doing work that you *have* to do rather than work that you *love* to do.

If you're considering whether or not to leave your present job, ask yourself which of the goals of the guerrilla entrepreneur are offered to you by your current position. Money? Maybe. Time? I doubt it. Health? Possibly, but not for sure. Bonding? Only with fellow employee-slaves. Longevity? Hardly; if current downsizing trends continue, you'll likely be let go just when you've got life all figured out.

I am not here to badmouth corporate America. I absolutely loved every single day of my sentence there. It's just that these postcorporate days are my good old days.

While writing this chapter, I've got to admit that I took time off to throw the tennis ball for my dog until my arm got tired, to take my one-mile walk through the forest next to my house, to make love to my wife, and to sample the curry sauce for the dinner we're having. These are not the things that distracted me during my corporate days. They are fringe benefits of being a guerrilla entrepreneur. I live in a constant state of euphoria.

This book has been written to get you to move to that state.

3

Measuring Success in
the 21st Century

SUCCESS AT WORK in the twenty-first century will be a lot
more fulfilling than success at work in the twentieth. People not
happy with their work in the twenty-first century will be doing
something wrong. If they're earning more money than they ever
imagined, but are not content, they most assuredly are not guerrilla successes. Success for the entrepreneur will be measured by
inner satisfaction more than any other criterion.

Perhaps that peace of soul can come from the work you do.
It could also come from your leisure time and your achieve-
ments. Most likely, it will be a combination, for a balanced
life blends work with play. You won't be happy all of the time. If
you were, you'd soon lose the edge necessary to succeed in a
highly competitive century, one in which *individuals* (rather
than huge corporations) will compete for time, attention, and
dollars. Guerrillas always have that edge. But guerrillas are
happy more often than not.

Inner satisfaction is something you get not by seeking it, but
by seeking work that ignites your passion and then doing that
work. It is a realization that occurs rather than a consciously
sought attainment. But you won't realize it by chasing money or
even by getting money, no matter how much you make.

Along with inner satisfaction, the guerrilla entrepreneur will
orient his business toward being with his family—the small nu-
clear family of the twentieth century as well as the larger, extended family of the twenty-first century. He will become part of
his community, whether that community is his neighborhood,
his industry, or his online world. He will obtain much of the fun

he needs from the work he does, but will recognize he needs recreation beyond work. Surely he will be motivated by the old goals of financial independence, control of his destiny, and recognition of his talents. But he will also be drawn to a newer goal best described as *innovation* or *discovery.* He will want to contribute to society with more than his time or money. Through the work he does, he will find ways to do this, because guerrillas are resourceful. In fact, resourcefulness is a survival technique of the guerrilla.

A guerrilla road map

The guerrilla entrepreneur is able to succeed on the journey by having a clear and simple road map. Guerrilla signposts illuminate the road. They say:

* Learn.
* Cooperate.
* Focus.
* Feel passion.
* Delegate.
* Share.
* Respect time.
* Bend.
* Profit.
* See.

These signposts enable guerrillas to select their pace and never lose their way. Guerrillas realize that even after they have passed a sign, they continue to move in the right direction. They keep in mind the words on these additional signposts:

* Plan.
* Manage.
* Market.
* Sell.
* Serve.
* Satisfy.
* Relate.
* Globalize.

* Improve.

* Be cool.

Since guerrillas strive to achieve inner satisfaction, the components of happiness are well known to them. In his book *The Pursuit of Happiness*, author David Myers, sounding a lot like a guerrilla, cites ten items that promote happiness: *What promotes happiness*

1. A fit and healthy body
2. Realistic goals and expectations
3. Positive self-esteem
4. Feelings of control
5. Optimism
6. Outgoingness
7. Supportive friendships
8. An intimate, sexually warm marriage of equals
9. Challenging work and active leisure coupled with adequate rest and retreat
10. Spiritual faith

We are living at a time when people are just beginning to turn down promotions, to quit the corporate rat race to start businesses for themselves, to move to less stressful environments, to pursue less demanding careers. People are taking a new look at the meaning of success. They no longer automatically assume that the only way to be successful is to be always moving up the corporate ladder, to be burning the midnight oil. An employee survey by Levi Strauss showed that 79 percent wanted more flexibility to set their own work schedules, "presumably," says a personnel director, "so they can spend more time with their families and pursue other interests."

Responding to a newspaper reporter's blunt question — "What makes people happy?" — randomly selected people at San Francisco's Fisherman's Wharf said what you'd expect of guerrillas. One woman said, "Success. Money enough to do everything you want. Liking what you're doing. Vacations. Good friends and good relationships. People to do things with and laugh with." Another woman added, "Being truly seen and accepted for who you are." A third said, "Feeling spiritually whole, knowing you haven't created disharmony. Materially taken care of." And a fourth said, "Success and security as the person defines it." One man felt that people are made happy by "a sense of contributing through a job, parenting, or a relationship with a spouse." Another man said it was "freedom from worry and a sense of having done something important. A sense of purpose by making a significant contribution."

These are lofty ideas—historically, we asked for only food, clothing, and shelter. Then came three revolutions—agricultural, industrial, and informational. We are now in a fourth revolution—the Creative Age. Disseminating so much information requires great creativity. Obviously, our goals have evolved too. They continue to evolve with time, and guerrillas evolve with them.

Not all American workers are tuned in to these changes. A recent Roper survey showed that only 18 percent of people feel that their careers are personally and financially rewarding. But we Americans are finally coming to our senses. People are learning how to gear down from the fast track, how to experience inner satisfaction in their careers.

Coming to our senses

A Robert Half International survey taken in 1996 indicated that two out of three respondents would be willing to reduce their work hours and salary by an average of 20.8 percent, up from 13 percent in 1989, in order to have more family and personal time. For the first time in sixteen years, Americans chose leisure (41 percent) over work (36 percent) as "the important thing" in life, according to a Roper survey. The survey showed that people of the 1990s are seeking "meaningful work" or "balance between work life and personal life."

And this trend is not limited to the United States. The concept of work outside the structure of a standard nine-to-five job is catching on worldwide. My books have been translated into thirty-five languages. I just returned from running a two-day marketing seminar in Indonesia. Which of my books was most intriguing to the good citizens of Jakarta? *Guerrilla Marketing for the Home-Based Business.*

In America, a whole new set of rules is emerging. To succeed in the past, all you had to do was follow orders and perform the same routine tasks day after day. In the future, and in the present, what you have to do is to identify and solve problems quickly.

Here is the first rule of the future: *Be prepared to change collars.* The man in the gray flannel suit with a white-collar job no longer has the job, eliminated due to the surgical elimination of layers of management. As I write this, three thousand people per day are being laid off in the United States. That same man, now without a job, doesn't wear a gray flannel suit anymore because the era of the technician is upon us, and technicians don't wear suits. He no longer wears a white collar because it is increasingly being recognized as garb of the past. And, most important, he is probably not a man in the first place since so many women are swelling the ranks of entrepreneurial America.

The first rule of the future

Jobs throughout America are disappearing like smoke in the wind, especially the high-paid, white-collar jobs held by men and women at the peak of their careers. The *New York Times* reports that nearly 75 percent of all households have had a close encounter with layoffs since 1980. In 33 percent of those cases, a family member lost a job. In nearly 40 percent, a relative, friend, or neighbor was laid off. One in ten adults, meaning nineteen million people, acknowledged that the lost job precipitated a major crisis.

You'd figure that such downsizing of companies and the overall labor force would occur during a recession. But these layoffs are occurring during an economic recovery that has lasted for five years, even at companies that are doing very well. The overall result is the most acute job insecurity since the Depression, producing an unrelenting angst that has shattered people's notions of work, self, and the promise of tomorrow. In the past, a layoff meant a temporary interruption in the job. Work would be slow, so a factory shift would be laid off; but these workers stayed near the phone, knowing it would inevitably ring with an invitation to return to work. But the phone rings no more. Today, a layoff means a permanent, irrevocable, painful goodbye. No wonder the time is so ripe for guerrilla entrepreneurs.

Just yesterday, America's economy was based on companies that made more and more of the same product at lower and lower prices. Today, the economy is based on companies that quickly provide customized products and services to meet the tailored needs of small groups of consumers. Fortunately, such an economy is a natural spawning ground for guerrilla entrepreneurs.

A spawning ground for guerrillas

Here is the second rule of the future: *Learn to love your network*. In the past, Americans would measure success by their ability to climb the corporate ladder. But that ladder exists no more. Success is measured by the results of your creativity, your autonomy, and your ability to devise a new solution, develop a new idea, deliver a new service. Often, success is achieved by teams. At the conclusion of a project, the teams disband and the people move to other teams. The ladder is now a network—an infinite number of paths that ultimately connect with many others. Rather than trudge from one rung to the next on a rigid upward course, you can connect with others at lightning speed and then disconnect when your purposes have been achieved. The larger your network, the more work will come your way. The better you treat other members of the network, the better they'll treat you. As in the past, people who are fun to work with will be at a premium. Prima donnas and mean-spirited high achievers need not apply in the world of the guerrilla entrepreneur.

It's a wired world

Here is the third rule of the future: *It's a wired world; deal with it*. The Internet is growing at a faster rate than TV grew during its fastest growth spurt. The Internet is a place for fun and profits, work and play, data and wisdom, love and friendship, networking and going it alone—a hotbed for guerrilla entrepreneurs. It allows people to send text, information, videos, graphics, and sound to almost any place on the planet. It operates in

154 nations already. A lot of work in the future will consist of collaborations strictly by computer network. The past four books I have written were co-authored by men who connected with me online only. After one initial face-to-face meeting, we created our books (*The Guerrilla Marketing Handbook* and *Guerrilla Marketing for the Home-Based Business* with Seth Godin, and *Guerrilla Marketing Online* and *Guerrilla Marketing Online Weapons* with Charles Rubin) via online communications. Easy as pie, very streamlined, a lot of fun, and timesaving, too. As I write of the future, I have one foot firmly planted in it. My commuting is done on the information superhighway.

We face three societal pressures today, says Andy Grove, the CEO of Intel Corporation, a Silicon Valley superstar: "Education, health, and commuting." And we are all now governed by Moore's Law: "Every eighteen months, computers double in power and therefore halve in cost," a trend that is putting the massive power of mainframe computers onto the desks of millions of entrepreneurs. In a wired world, fewer people directly manufacture products, while more people think of ways to make the products more valuable through design, marketing, or engineering.

Here is the fourth rule of the future: *What you earn depends more than ever upon what you learn.* You can do your learning at college, technical school, or training on the job. In California, enrollment in community colleges has soared by 300 percent in the past three decades. A woman with a community college degree earns 33 percent more than her counterpart with only a high school diploma. For men, the figure is 26 percent more money. Security no longer comes from sticking with one company for an entire career, but by maintaining a portfolio of flexible skills. That is why so many universities now offer lifelong learning classes, serving students from college age through golden age. The new economy will not be a dog-eat-dog economy, but a skill-eat-skill economy. The more skills you have and the better trained you are at the skills you have, the more success you will achieve. Pure cause and effect.

A skill-eat-skill economy

In Search of Excellence author Tom Peters calls guerrilla

entrepreneurs to action: "The only way to lose is not to try. Not every big firm is a Wal-Mart or a CNN. Not every firm will be around by the year 2000. But the trend is unmistakable. Frankly, I don't know how to do much more than exhort, 'Build your own firm, create your own network'—it's that or bust."

Says Peters of the future, "Add it up and you get something rather surprising. There's no rejection of the past in all this! Expertise is more important than ever, not less. And bigness has its place. However, expertise is being changed, altered almost beyond recognition. If you're not skilled/motivated/passionate about something, you're in trouble!" Notice this—the man did not say what you're to be skilled or motivated or passionate *Care like crazy*   about—that's for you to determine. He only advises that you *care like crazy* about it.

Deepak Chopra, author of *Ageless Body, Timeless Mind*, also speaks of what you should care like crazy about. He suggests simply that you ask yourself, "If I had all the time and money in the world, what would I do?" If you persist in asking that question, the answer will come to you, and when it tells you what it is, then *do that thing*. He says that if you do, you will have all the money and time that you will ever need.

Chopra, who also wrote *The Seven Spiritual Laws of Success*, offers this advice to would-be guerrilla entrepreneurs, and I wish I could print it in neon ink for you: "There is one thing each of us has that no one else has. There is one thing you can do that nobody else can. Find it, and foster it. You will never die at your business if you are doing what you are meant to do."

Merely doing it is the start to achieving success in the twenty-first century.

4

Integrating Your Business with Your Life

ONE OF THE MOST pleasurable yet difficult tasks for a guerrilla entrepreneur to achieve and maintain is living in the moment. You've got to begin that task right now, as you read this book, if you're to become an entrepreneur of the guerrilla persuasion. To do so, you'll have to let go of your old notions of work and leisure. It will mean dismantling those compartments into which you, or more likely, your great-grandparents, have divided your life.

In doing this, you'll free yourself to do things that matter to you. If you're a spiritual person and you get in touch with the God within you at church, the synagogue, the temple, or while reading the Bible, you'll be able to be your spiritual self whenever and wherever you want. If you want to spend more time with your family, you'll be able to. One of the greatest rewards of being an entrepreneur in the coming century will be the chance for people to recognize the pure nobility of work when it is pursued with joy rather than obligation. But work in the future will not be an obsession as it is right now. It will be part of a well-balanced existence. You will have many better things to do than work. Oscar Wilde once said, "Work is the refuge of people who have nothing better to do."

When a friend of mine, Liz Hymans, rows a raft through the thundering rapids of the Colorado River at the bottom of the Grand Canyon and then shoots photographs from the banks where she sleeps under the stars—she is working. She is getting paid for the rowing and for the photography. Would she do these things even if she was not getting paid? That's the right question. *How Liz Hymans works*

And Liz has the right answer—yes. When my colleague Orvel Ray Wilson captivates and motivates an audience of salespeople with a performance worthy of stage or screen, is his motivation the money? You'd think it is, but the answer is no. He would probably pay for the privilege of having so much fun helping people succeed.

Liz and Orvel Ray have integrated their businesses with their lives. It's not that easy to draw the line between their work and their leisure. They planned it that way. And they seem to smile a lot. I wonder if there's a cause and effect. I know there is.

My wife, Pat, loves kids, loves art, loves playing. To integrate what she loves to do with making a living, she went to graduate school in counseling and psychology and now pulls in big dollars as a pediatric art and play therapist in a major hospital. Even better, she works only three afternoons a week. When people have a hard time telling when you are working and when you are having fun, you're doing something right. It's a sign that you're living in a substantial number of precious moments. Work may not always be pure enjoyment for the guerrilla entrepreneur, but it will be a lot of the time. In today's workplace, work is rarely enjoyable to the worker. At one time there wasn't a way out. There is now.

Step back a few paces   Now entrepreneurial guerrillas are stepping back a few paces and seeing that work is not the entire picture. Other parts of that picture include recreation, friends, family, faith, health, location, education, travel, and free time. Have I left anything out? Probably. It's a big and beautiful picture. These are the rewards of living. The rewards should not be reserved for your retirement because guerrillas never completely retire from work. They may cut back, but they're having too much of a blast to retire. As guerrillas, they want to use their longevity for meeting and savoring the elixir of surmounting new challenges as times, technology, and they themselves undergo staggering changes. As much as they feel passion for their work, guerrilla entrepreneurs never allow it to erode the other joys of living. The elixir recipe calls for enjoying life while earning a living.

Luckily, more people are climbing out of the full-time em-

ployment mire and discovering that there is life and work beyond a standard job. The French refer to *le troisième age*, "the
third age," life beyond the job. To them, the first age is growing
up. The second is working. The third is life beyond the job.

The third age

Guerrilla entrepreneurs plan and arrange their lives so that
these second and third ages run concurrently. They also realize
that the first age runs for a lifetime if they go about things in the
right way. The third age is not retirement. Unlike retirement, it
is a time for fulfillment. It is not brief like retirement. It lasts
from the beginning of working until the end of living. It is not
only for older people. It is not characterized by boredom, and
certainly not by a shortage of funds.

People living in the third age seek customers instead of jobs,
seek solutions to problems rather than employment. They don't
have a single kind of work that generates income, but rather a
portfolio of work. They do, as London Business School professor
Charles Handy says, "some things for money, some because they
interest [them], some out of love or kindness, and some for the
sheer hell of it." They easily integrate these activities into their
lives. Who would want to miss travel, discovery, learning, earning, improving, teaching, and giving?

As businesses come to grips with the ugly fact that offices are
idle about 75 percent of the time, they are forcing people into
the third age. Because of the ability to transfer information so
quickly by modem, phone, or fax machine, there is no longer a
need for everyone to be in the same place at the same time. As
this happens, the power of the individual increases. Why pay
rent for an office when you can take a drive in the country in a
car equipped with a fax machine, a phone, and a laptop computer? Technology makes it easier than ever to integrate work
with life. Once you cozy up to it, technology also makes this
integration faster and a lot more fun.

More and more companies are becoming what are called
80–20 firms. That means that only 20 percent of the people
involved in production or service are actually employed by the
company. The rest will be freelancers, part-timers, third-agers,
guerrilla entrepreneurs. There will be a lot of work for these

80–20 firms

people. Specialists and temporary workers will be in high demand. The fact is, we're rapidly reaching the point at which companies have more part-time employees outside the organization than full-time employees inside.

These changes are green lights for guerrillas. As full-time jobs become more scarce and portfolio jobs increase, people who realize that they can integrate their work with their lives are finding that opportunities abound. Americans are finally discovering that they do not have to build a huge fire. Instead, they are building smaller fires and finding them much easier to tend.

Because of their portfolios of work, guerrilla entrepreneurs have an automatic safeguard against burnout. That safeguard is called change. It's not easy to change your life when you have a full-time job that is disconnected from your life. But change is at your fingertips and at your command when you have a selection of work skills, a variety of income sources. Supposedly, people live a lifetime utilizing only 25 percent of their talents. Guerrilla entrepreneurs utilize far more, digging into that untapped 75 percent and finding it a lucrative source of income and pleasure. They know which skills can be blended with their other pursuits in life, and they focus upon these skills, aiming for integration.

When they enjoy their leisure, guerrillas are not piddling away their time, though they know there is absolutely nothing wrong with the joy of nonaccomplishment. Instead, most of their leisure involves an activity that produces satisfaction, offers control, and does not upset the balance in their lives. Guerrilla entrepreneurs know well that leisure has a regenerative, therapeutic quality.

Ten guerrilla attitudes

In order to integrate your business with your life, exactly what do you need? You must have ten attitudes and ten pieces of real equipment. These are the ten attitudes:

1. Organization
2. Determination
3. Discipline
4. Passion
5. Love of life

6. Optimism
7. Flexibility
8. Honesty
9. Self-esteem
10. Generosity

What is the cost of these ten attitudes? The only cost is giving up old ideas, old habits, and old weaknesses. The cost of the ten pieces of real equipment is about $5,000, and you don't need all the equipment at first. These are the ten items:

1. Computer
2. Printer
3. Modem
4. Software
5. Fax machine
6. Telephone
7. Answering device
8. Cellular telephone
9. Scanner
10. Phone lines for your phone, computer, and fax machine

You will also incur, in the integration of your work into your life, continuing charges. You will be responsible for five important fees. Do not be tempted to skimp on these fees, because that might mean skimping on your chances of success. These are the five fees:

1. Monthly marketing
2. Online service charges
3. Taxes
4. Insurance
5. Rental of equipment, space, and office furniture

Armed with these attitudes and this equipment, you will be primed for success.

However, even after attaining these prerequisites for contentment and fortune as a guerrilla, you must also be armed with critical knowledge of your limitations. Don't overextend your-

*No shoddiness
allowed*

self, because you cannot allow even a trace of amateurism or shoddiness to creep into your business. Guerrilla entrepreneurs have wide-ranging networks of people whom they can turn to when they need help. Their Rolodexes are brimming with names of talented independent contractors, usually fellow guerrilla entrepreneurs. Best of all, they achieve better results using these nonemployees than they would with their own employees, because the cream of the crop opts for the life of an independent contractor; their ranks swell with previously highly paid executives who saw the light and left the corporate womb. In most cases, you get far more than what you pay for when you link up with carefully selected independent contractors.

One term used to describe businesses run by guerrilla entrepreneurs is "virtual corporations." Frequently one-person operations, these businesses use the technology I've listed to grow quickly and efficiently with minimal expense. Virtual corporations generally have no employees, no factories, no fancy offices, no high overheads, no sales staff, and no unnecessary expenses. Instead, they have freedom, flexibility, and efficiency. Thus, they increase their revenues and not their expenses.

*Simplicity of
work style*

People who run virtual corporations say that such simplicity of work style enables them to concentrate on what they do best. When I was a creative director in one of the world's largest advertising agencies, I was paid to be creative, but I spent a lot of my time being administrative, the result of having a staff of forty people. I accomplished then only a fraction of what I accomplish now. Running a virtual corporation, you will be forced to clearly understand your core business. You will be the person in control of your destiny; you won't share the credit for your successes or the blame for your failures.

The ideal virtual corporation reduces the distance between the entrepreneur and the customer, the entrepreneur and his family, the entrepreneur and her life's goals. It blends work with life in nearly perfect harmony.

Guerrillas' businesses thrive as virtual companies. They embrace the technology that allows them this freedom, and then they prosper in their businesses and the other important aspects of their lives. It wasn't always as easy to run a virtual company. If it was, you'd have learned about being a guerrilla entrepreneur from your grandparents. They also would have loved the benefits of integrating their business with their lives. But they didn't have the choice that you do.

5

Maintaining Balance

ALTHOUGH I WISH to make the life of a guerrilla entrepreneur sound interesting, challenging, and rewarding to you — I wish to lead you not into temptation, but to deliver you from evil.

The temptation will be success. When it comes, you're going to be nuts about it, and you'll want more of it — the deluxe version. Go for it. But don't go with so much gusto that you destroy the balance in your life.

The evil will be in your reactions to success. You may become solely motivated by the high profits that come with being an effective entrepreneur. You might change focus from the path of the guerrilla to the path of the work slave. Or, worst of all, you might continue working without a plan.

Balance is the key to keeping temptations and evils at bay. It is the critical difference between a guerrilla entrepreneur and a traditional entrepreneur. A guerrilla knows that unless balance is part of the overall plan — right from the start — it's only going to be a word and never a style of living. Balance is very difficult to achieve if it's something you figure you'll get down the road. If you were on a high wire, balance is not something you'd settle for *eventually*. You'd want it always. You'd want it now. Life in the twenty-first century will be a high wire.

Five kinds of work

Guerrillas not only balance their work time with leisure time, learning time, family time, and time for anything else they want to do — they also balance their work time itself. And they've learned that there are five kinds of work:

1. *Wage work* is job work in this scenario. You sell your time to the company employing you, and they manage your time. At one time, this work made the most sense for people. Your grandparents lived during that time, but it has passed. Wage work is nonsense for over half the people doing it now.

2. *Fee work* is professional work. Professionals in many fields charge a fee for the work they do and for their time—which is then spent the way they want, when they want, under their own management. People who work as consultants for businesses charge fees; they don't earn wages. This makes the businesses *and* the professional individuals satisfied.

3. *Housework* is the work done on and for the home. It's work that has to be done, such as cooking, cleaning, and shopping, and is ordinarily unpaid. These days, it is rapidly being redistributed from women to men. At the same time, it is more appreciated and is important enough to be part of a well-balanced work portfolio.

4. *Study work* is educational work. Self-improvement by way of an advanced degree or extra certification is more important than ever, as more people discover that a second or third degree gives them an edge in the working world. Guerrillas study to improve in many areas aside from work. Human understanding is part of what they learn.

5. *Volunteer work* is free work. You do this work for causes such as schools, hospitals, religious groups, political groups, charities, and sports groups. The income you derive from this work is emotional, spiritual, and permanent. To many people, it is more gratifying than financial income.

Guerrillas try to engage in all five kinds of work, knowing the benefits of each one will help them maintain balance. Wage work offers security; fee work provides the joy of being paid for your talent and knowledge; housework keeps you grounded; study work is an investment in yourself; volunteer work is the taxes paid by your body to your soul.

How can you possibly fit all five kinds of work into your life?

It's easy when you *plan at the outset.* Planning is a built-in balance-provider. It helps ensure that you'll have time to help at home, to learn about life, and to help others while you bring home the bacon with your other pursuits—a regular gig a few days a week or even once month. If you do too much of any one kind of work, you'll be out of balance, and the work will almost instantly cease to be much fun. In the twenty-first century, guerrilla entrepreneurs will achieve balance as a matter of choice, not as a matter of necessity.

Who leads the way in living unbalanced lives? Workaholics top the list; they often believe that unless they do their work immediately, the universe will come to a grinding halt. High achievers who sacrifice freedom come next on the list of the unbalanced; they intentionally abandon balance for the sake of fame or fortune. Fame and fortune do have their price, but balance need not be part of it. Kids grow up only once. If you miss it the first time, there's no rerun.

Factory workers in the latter half of the twentieth century have worked an average of forty hours per week. Unskilled laborers typically work only forty. But business owners average fifty-nine hours of work per week. What did these business owners have in mind when they opened their businesses? Certainly not a balanced structure for their work time and their free time. Certainly not an understanding of balance in life.

Some experts believe that workaholics are dying faster than alcoholics. This may not be readily apparent because so many workaholics watch their nutrition and exercise. They look great and may even work out regularly, but that only prolongs their ability to remain workaholics. They aren't listening to their bodies telling them something is wrong, so it takes something like a massive coronary to get their attention.

Guerrilla entrepreneurs are exceptional listeners. They listen to their customers, to their mentors, to their friends, and to their kids. They listen to their parents and certainly to their teachers. They also listen to their bodies, their inner voice, the voice of reason. They never allow the past to dictate the future.

In the past world of work, balance had no part, just as the idea of having enough time was not appreciated until the late 1980s. Yet although the idea of balance is finally on the forefront of the American mind, it is still a clouded notion, still a new concept, still considered an unattainable dream to many people. As one who has maintained balance for twenty-five years and not found it very difficult, I believe that only two factors are required to achieve balance: to *imagine* it, and then to *commit* to it. Imagining it was harder than committing to it for me. Once I had visualized it, it was a relative cinch to commit to it.

This idea of visualizing balance is more "old age" than "new age." It is found in ancient scriptural texts of India. These writings state that success can be achieved effortlessly. Within every desire lie the mechanics of its fulfillment, its accomplishment. Wishing can breathe life into them. If I had read that before I had lived it, I would have thought it was nonsense. Now I think it's common sense.

As water automatically seeks its own level, intentions automatically seek their fulfillment if left alone. I'm not referring to the narrow intention of making a zillion bucks. Instead, I mean the broader intentions that define who you are—such as the intention to lead a balanced life. Keep in mind that nature's *Nature's* intelligence is far superior to the rational thought of human *intelligence* beings. Trees and fish, insects and star systems have successfully adapted to existence a lot longer than we have.

Most people spend 99 percent of their time engaged in judgment, in labeling other people and their activities. If you stop doing that, you can begin to get in touch with your own potential—and that potential sure doesn't call for you to work for others forty hours a week *or* to work for yourself fifty-nine hours a week.

So don't be too narrow in your focus. The cost of wanting a result that is too specific is often stress and heart attacks. In America, by the time a person gets to the top, he's divorced, his kids are a mess, and his private life is in shambles. This is called success, but the person is miserable. Success should guarantee happiness as well. Does that make sense to you? It makes sense to me. What doesn't make sense is why financial success and emotional happiness so rarely coexist.

To hit what you aim at, keep your attention on the present, and orient yourself to the *process,* not to the *outcome.* If you focus on providing the finest product or the finest service, instead of concentrating solely on the bottom line, you will live according to your plan.

If your focus broadens to include doing what you love during leisure time, family time, and other nonwork time, your plan will come vibrantly alive, and you will see clearly what you must do to keep it alive. My weekends have started on Wednesday after work, at around 6:00 P.M. Experiencing the glory of a four-day weekend, the options for recreation, and the benefits to my family—not to mention the bliss I find in working at home—I found it relatively simple to maintain this balance, through good times and bad. Once you step into paradise, it is not human nature to step out.

One of the most valuable requisites for creating balance is flexibility. Even as I tell you that I work three days a week, I know good and well that I'll be flying to Toronto this Thursday and speaking all day Friday. What about my three-day week? Out the window, that's what. *Almost* all my weeks are three-day weeks, but if I didn't have the flexibility to work five or seven days when the situation demanded my time, I'd be no guerrilla.

Living and working a balanced life means knowing how to handle periods of imbalance and uncertainty that characterize growth and beginning new ventures. Quentin Tarantino, the movie director, upon completing his acclaimed film *Pulp Fiction,* said, "It was like entering a smoky room, then proceeding forward on faith even though I didn't see where I was going. Strictly faith kept me moving forward until the smoke began to vanish and I could see everything clearly." He gave up perfect balance, experienced the uncertainty, but, guided by his faith in himself and his intentions, he emerged with a sense of clarity and regained his balance.

Skiing is like that—it includes the sense of a controlled

The smoky room

fall and feeling slightly out of balance almost all the time; yet you always catch yourself, restore your balance, and proceed at breakneck speed, propelled by gravity and faith in your ability. While you're skiing, there is certainly no time for drawn-out rational thought. Often, regaining balance means moving fifty-eight sets of muscles in less than a quarter of a second. You can't think that through. Your body takes all its cues from your overall *intention*. Unless that intention is firmly planted in your heart and mind before you begin, you will find it very difficult to acquire it once you've established momentum. The idea is to maintain the momentum and to make balance part of the package.

You'll find it relatively easy to maintain balance if you begin with it. Start with it *no matter what.* Don't delude yourself into thinking you can switch gears later. Many have tried. Most have failed. Guerrillas are so enamored with the idea of balance that they wouldn't dream of losing sight of their target before they let the arrows fly. They know that once the arrows are in full flight, you can't say to them, "Okay, hang a left turn now!"

As a guerrilla entrepreneur, you're shooting an arrow. You get to take aim in any direction you want. If that direction does not include balance, you'll misfire. You will not be following the way of the guerrilla.

You realize by now that being a guerrilla entrepreneur is far more than pure work. It's really a work style, a lifestyle, a living style, a behavior style, a values style, a priorities style.

If you don't have leisure activities that you love as much as your work, if you don't have a family or relationships that you enjoy every bit as much as your work, if you don't have the time to engage in leisure or bask in relationships, you're no guerrilla. For those are the elements that provide balance. You need them for equilibrium as much as you need the work itself.

Loving your leisure

6

The Yardstick for Measuring
the Success of a Business

THE FIRST FACTOR in measuring the success of your business is to assess your inner satisfaction, to determine whether you are enjoying the process of being in business or even enjoying being alive. The second factor is to ascertain that your business meshes as well with your life as it does with your essence — who you really are. The third factor is to determine whether or not you have balance in your life.

And there's a fourth measurement of your success — *after* you've arranged to have enough free time, *after* you've found ways to contribute to your planet, *after* you've formed your connections, *after* your relationships are in order and your health is excellent. This measuring method should be part of your overall plan, or you'll lose your way.

The yardstick to which I refer is *profits*, the lifeblood of a business. Guerrillas keep their eyes on that bottom line, but they never lose their awareness of their higher priorities.

Amazingly, some businesses *never* address this crucial yardstick. Even more ridiculous, many businesses make this the *only* criterion of their success. The way of the guerrilla gives this measure of success a modified priority. Guerrilla entrepreneurs are inevitably interested in this measurement because it is an important part of why they are in business in the first place. But they never give profits the highest priority because profits are neither the only nor the most important reason for being in business.

More important than profits

Here are ten things that true guerrilla entrepreneurs consider to be more important than profits:

1. Their future
2. Their overall plan
3. Their customers
4. Their employees
5. Their prospects
6. Their families
7. Their time
8. Their inner satisfaction
9. Their integration of business and life
10. Their balance

Here are ten things that true guerrilla entrepreneurs consider less important than profits:

Less important than profits

1. Their sales
2. Their turnover
3. Their response rate
4. Their store traffic
5. Their volume
6. Their gross
7. Their press coverage
8. Their ego
9. Their status quo
10. Their growth

The thousands of workers laid off each year in this country represent *families* who have lost their security—families displaced by companies finally facing up to the reality of profits. If more companies went the way of the guerrilla and put less of a premium on the almighty profit, more families would be spared the pain of layoffs.

For what are profits? They are what is left over after the business expenses have been paid. In reality, they are whatever the business owner *determines* them to be. Is that leased Porsche the owner's personal financial responsibility, allowing the profits to remain high—or is it a business expense that is deducted from the profits? The owner's answer determines her profit margin.

Until the 1980s, the American business community clung to

tradition instead of facing the business of new realities, costs of goods, and standards in wages. It stuck to outmoded business methods that it would have replaced in an instant if it had read figures other than the bottom line. But reality has a way of making itself known, often by the sound of the bill collector pounding on the door or the collection agency calling on the phone. So American business had to become mean in order to be lean.

Their meanness began with the lopping off of an entire layer of middle management.

Because someone was oblivious to the role of profits in a company—more important than sales, leads, and responses to advertising—a lot of bright, hard-working people lost their jobs, and in many cases, their identities as well. Social workers in all fifty states will tell you that job loss is a concomitant of spousal abuse, alcoholism, substance abuse, suicide, child beating, divorce—a grim list. *Grim* also describes the situation of financially healthy companies that eventually were beset with money problems: during the days of largesse, employees wasted time huddling at the water cooler, doing unnecessary work, passing paperwork around, writing memos that didn't have to be written, going to meetings that didn't have to be held, and working mindlessly and desperately to justify the fact that they were drawing a paycheck. Eventually these companies had to pay the piper. Who was kidding whom?

In the beginning, it seemed the businesses were being kidded. They were losing money at record-breaking paces, forcing the ones that didn't go bankrupt (and they did go into Bankruptcy Law Chapters 7, 11, or 13 in record numbers) to become the size they should have been in the first place—smaller, much smaller. This downsizing became known as right-sizing because it was the right size all along. But American business had a mis-begotten notion, borrowed from the dinosaurs—and you know what happened to them—that large is good and humongous might be even better. By allowing unnecessary employees to do unnecessary work and spend unnecessary time doing it, busi-

Borrowed from the dinosaurs

nesses discovered that their profits were being eroded away and even their reserves were being tapped.

Once these businesses learned that they were being fooled, they began their mass firings—or, more delicately stated, layoffs. Whether the result of a firing, a layoff, or a downsizing, the pain for those asked to leave remains the same. It's a pain unknown to guerrillas because they never lose sight of that bottom line, never allow anything to eat away at their profits unnecessarily.

Downsizing came from cost cutting, from tactics to gain efficiency, from companies wishing to boost their stock prices, from firms hoping to be more competitive in the global arena. But in most cases, the shrinking of the payroll was a choice between purging and becoming extinct.

"To keep people employed on a long-term basis, you have to do some painful things," said the chief executive officer of one of Silicon Valley's superstar companies. "Otherwise, there won't be any jobs at all." Says a chief financial officer of a huge bank, "You can't keep on artificially employing people who aren't needed." Pan-American World Airways downsized themselves right out of existence. After the bloodbath was over, there wasn't enough of Pan-Am left to pay the bills.

What happened to all those people who were downsized out of a job? And what was the effect on the overall job picture? The big corporate jobs disappeared forever, as they will continue to for a long time. A full 90 percent of the new jobs came from entrepreneurs, giving rise to a growth spurt of new small businesses. In 1995, over 2 million of them were formed. In 1994, the number had been 1.8 million. The trend is clear.

Will all those entrepreneurs survive? They will not. Only the guerrilla entrepreneur will be prepared for the new workplace of the twenty-first century, the business owner who understands profits right from the beginning. As with balance, if you have a clear grasp of what it takes to make profits before you even begin, you will probably maintain that clarity for the life of your business.

Guerrilla entrepreneurs emphasize profitability and are

thus never forced into a downsizing mode, never have to lay off employees en masse, never force employees into that pathetic state of insecurity, never have to inflict the pains caused by bottom-line negligence.

They manage to do this because they never kid themselves. They know that big isn't necessarily better, that expensive isn't necessarily worth the extra expense. They perform two primary jobs that increase their profits:

* They improve everything they do.
* They eliminate any mistakes entirely.

Guerrillas have a wide definition of *everything*—it consists of anything connected with their business, inside and out. They have an equally broad definition of *mistakes*. Anything that is not done with excellence is a mistake. Guerrillas are not perfectionists, knowing that perfectionists cause stress for others and can be ineffective in their use of time. But guerrillas do have high standards and noble expectations. They expect those standards to be met without exception. They take for granted that their expectations will be met and often exceeded.

The guerrilla entrepreneur knows that improvements increase profits and that mistakes decrease profits.

What do the corporate instigators of the downsizing era have to say about their reprehensible but unavoidable behavior? "It was one of the hardest things I've ever done. I felt like I was personally contributing to the recession," says the CEO of a large software company. If he had to do it over, he "would have hired at a more conservative rate. I would have planned fewer projects, and I would have focused and done a few things well."

Right now (a clear indication that the time is right for entrepreneurs to become guerrillas, flourish, and succeed), almost half of all U.S. workers are employed in industries that are shedding jobs, and the public sector is also cutting back. For every person put out of work because of the cyclical nature of the economy—being fired, quitting, or retiring—*three* are cut as corporations restructure. Those corporations have made their mistakes before. They are not going to make them again.

Does cost cutting really help profitability? Of course it does, but the price is *inhumanity to people.* Companies that have laid off tens of thousands of workers, eliminated cost-sucking divisions, and allowed technology to save money for them have discovered consistently increasing profits each quarter. What do you suppose might have happened if they had seriously taken stock of their size and growth plans at the outset? They would have been spared the necessity of firing the people who had helped them grow. They would have spared themselves a fortune by doing without departments they shouldn't have had in the first place. They would have started out in a profit mode, committed themselves to that mode, and remained in that mode.

The price of cost cutting

Guerrilla entrepreneurs will live in that mode from day one. They will never allow the temptations of bigness to cause their profit curve to head south. They will avoid the overstaffing, obsolete technology, outmoded business techniques, and keeping-up-with-the-Joneses mentality that got their predecessors into trouble.

These guerrillas take into account the heartlessness of layoffs, so they keep their number of employees realistic, keep their focus on both humanity and profitability.

I play in a poker game each Monday night. We play one game in which players may purchase a card that is facing up. They can pay as much for that card as there is money in the pot, even more money if they want the card enough. Sometimes, there is $50 in the pot, but a player will pay $60 for the card, knowing ahead of time that he may have to split the pot with someone else. That player doesn't clearly understand the main point of poker, which is to make money.

That player is so intent on *winning* half the pot that his focus is diverted from the profits at the end of the rainbow. Guerrilla entrepreneurs love to win, but they know deep in their hearts that if you lose money, you don't win.

7

Sharing Your Profits Generously

IN THE LAST CHAPTER we investigated profits in terms of financial gain; in this chapter, we're going to switch mental gears, open our souls, and view profits from a wider perspective.

There is a business profit other than money: the joy of accomplishment, something that most employees of the twentieth century are deprived of, but something that transcends income. Money is one type of payment for work well done; praise and recognition provide a different kind of payment. Successes should be shared with suppliers, independent contractors, others in your network, and certainly employees. Profits should be shared with your community, your industry, your city, your nation. Rewards should be used to support the arts, education, the environment, charities that you care about, the needy. Think in terms of sharing your largesse with the planet. This will add momentum to your business profile while contributing to the betterment of humankind.

Profit-sharing will take on a vastly expanded meaning in the twenty-first century as participation in community becomes a criterion for success in business. Entrepreneurs are already learning that social responsibility and environmental awareness form part of the bottom line, along with all those dollars and cents. Warmth toward fellow beings is also part of it. Many a person would happily have the recognition for a job well done more than merely the money.

Tom's of Maine, a twenty-first-century kind of company that exists in the twentieth century, states its attitude toward employees in its mission statement: "To provide meaningful work, fair compensation, and a safe, healthy work environment that encourages openness, creativity, self-discipline and growth." Tom's of Maine's mission statement also includes serving and satisfying the following groups (notice that none are necessarily stockholders): customers, coworkers, owners, agents, suppliers, and the community in Maine and around the globe. Tom's dispenses its profits in the form of rewards both tangible and intangible: cash bonuses and pats on the back. Tom's recognizes the power of such recognition.

The power of recognition

That recognition can come in many forms, not just money and words of praise, award plaques and titles, corner offices and assistants. The profits that come in the form of repeat business, referral business, growth from within, and respect from the community or industry should be shared with anyone who even slightly contributed to them. The guerrilla entrepreneur's mindset is characterized by *wanting* to share, to let others stand in the spotlight, to spread the benefits.

This attitude is not merely the glowing realization that the more you give, the more you get; it isn't centered on payoffs to the business owner. The idea underlying generosity in an entrepreneurial sense is the powerful glue of *shared values*.

A guerrilla entrepreneur's employees, associates, network members, and service providers all have similar priorities in life. Money is not the only carrot on the stick. Because you understand and share these priorities, you can reward these people with free time, new responsibilities, invitations to be creative, license to innovate, tickets to events they'd appreciate, stock options, awards recognizing accomplishment, referrals to help their businesses, testimonial letters, good advice, fun, and friendship. If your values match those of the people who connect with your portfolio of careers, sharing those values will be standard operating procedure. Like the guerrilla, you will see that *sharing is a privilege* and not an obligation.

Other carrots on the stick

The guerrilla entrepreneur fuels profits and people by allowing employees and networkers to innovate for her own company as well as for their own sake. The wider you open the doors of creativity, the more big ideas will emerge.

In spite of many who cling to the past, sharing will come to be recognized as far more noble than vast personal gain, as our society evolves. Wealth will again be measured, as it was long ago among many Native American tribes, not as a matter of how much you've got but how much you give. Businesses will be run not only for profits, but also for the good of people.

Guerrilla entrepreneur Tom Chappell, founder and CEO of Tom's of Maine, says, "We expect priests and teachers, artists and naturalists, to care for and celebrate the human spirit. Shouldn't we expect the same from CEOs?"

Celebrating the human spirit

Those connected with your success should be provided with the data, facilities, and opportunities to learn and grow with you as you achieve more and more. They should see *your* growth as *their* growth, your success as theirs. When this happens, you will understand the glory of sharing. "What's in it for me?" will have been replaced by "What's in it for them?"

In order to share the profits generously, you've got to be keenly attuned to what your people want. Because you're a guerrilla entrepreneur, "your people" will probably mean not only employees, but rather every single individual who comes into contact with your company.

The art of knowing what people want will abet your enterprise; it will help you attract the people you need—the best prospects, the best customers, the best employees, the best PR people, the best mentors, the best independent contractors, the best suppliers, the best financial institutions, the best professionals, the best partners for strategic alliances. Research into the human spirit will enlighten you concerning people's real desires.

Offering pure joys

Rather than offering mere fees or salaries as in yestercentury, guerrillas will be offering pure joys—discovery, creativity, freedom, responsibility, self-realization, and the delight of being connected with a radiant success and making a meaningful contribution to society, the future, kids, parents, and business owners.

I give talks based on books that I've written. A person might come up to me and say, "I really enjoyed your book *Guerrilla*

Marketing. It was a delight to read and it taught me many important things. Thank you for writing it." That would make me feel good. Another might come up and say, "I thoroughly appreciated hearing your talk about guerrilla marketing. I found it fascinating and it affirmed many of the things I've always believed about marketing. You're a fine speaker." That would also make me feel good. A third person might say, "Five years ago, I read *Guerrilla Marketing*. Today, my business is ten times the size it was before I read that book." I would give myself a high five! I'd leap up and click my heels! I'd shout, "Yesssssssssss! That makes me feel great!" That's why I write books and talk about them. Not for the money. Not for the recognition. I do it to help people. And when it works out that I actually do help them, *that's* my reward. That's my profit. That's the carrot at the end of the stick.

Of course, I'm certainly grateful to anyone who liked the book or the talk, especially to anyone who told me they did, but those were only the means toward the end, and the end was the guerrilla with the business that grew by 1,000 percent. The book and the talk were necessary for that guerrilla's success. That success, shared with me, was profit-sharing of the highest degree.

Profit-sharing of the highest degree

Guerrilla entrepreneurs are innovative in how they share their bounty. Some use their generosity to express gratitude to employees as well as to improve their company. I know of one who takes his employees on a white-water raft trip, paid for by the company. He does it as an act of appreciation, but also to help foster teamwork among employees and to strengthen their relationships. Another guerrilla jets his employees to Hawaii for a week, encourages them to bring the whole family, puts them up in a luxury condo, and furnishes a car, all expenses paid. Everyone is happy, and it is no coincidence that the generous guerrilla runs a travel service that specializes in condominium vacations.

Profit-sharing in the next century will be characterized by rewards that radiate from the act itself. The travel service guerrilla benefited because he helped train better-informed employees. The employees benefited because they got a free Hawaiian holiday with their families. The condo management benefited because it will get positive word-of-mouth recommendations, warming up the relationship between the guerrilla and the condo owner. The airline benefited because it transported many people to and from Hawaii, setting the stage for a possible strategic alliance with the travel service. Hawaii benefited as a state with an important tourism industry. All this happened because a guerrilla knew how to be generous with his profits.

It's not very difficult to see that the people attracted to guerrilla entrepreneurship will be those who don't mind sharing. The entrepreneur of the twenty-first century will know that the *The backbone* backbone of any business is its people and that those people *of any business* aren't necessarily going to be her employees. Instead, they will be a wide variety of people. Knowledge of what those people want paves the way for the guerrilla. Along with that knowledge must come a talent at listening—and caring.

Listening and caring are not tough talents to develop if you are genuinely interested in people. An interest in people will be mandatory for the guerrilla entrepreneur, for the age of the lone wolf entrepreneur is well behind us. The more dependent you are, the better equipped you will be to prosper and flourish in a business of your own in the coming millennium.

You will be dependent upon customers, to be sure, but the range of your dependency will be far broader than that of entrepreneurs who have preceded you. You will probably depend, for information if not for something else, on others on the Internet. You will also depend on your family for helping to keep your working environment—possibly your home—conducive to accomplishment.

Interdependence   *Interdependence* will be a byword of the twenty-first century because of improved communications technology and a huge growth spurt in the number of independent workers. They will relate to each other, not as employee to employer, but as human to human, each making life a little easier for the other. The giving of rewards will become commonplace as society replaces one *g* word—*greed*—with another—*generosity*. Enlightened companies in today's society are asking what they can give, rather than take. Those companies freely give seminars, clinics, consultations, estimates, brochures, videos, samples, demonstrations, tours, test drives, trial uses, installation, and online hours.

Enlightened individuals in tomorrow's society will ask what they can give to others and will come up with answers such as time, money, recognition, a special parking space, a larger office, improved technology, connection to an existing network, responsibility, a club membership, a new title—the list continues and will be enlarged.

The guerrilla entrepreneur seeks these rewards—not to keep, but to give; not to own, but to grant. The mindset of giving will lead us out of the gimme-gimme-gimme past and into the better-to-give-than-receive future.

8

Money in the Coming Millennium

MONEY IS *not* the root of all evil. What George Bernard Shaw really said is that *lack of money* is the root of all evil. And what the Bible actually says is that the *love of money* is the root of all evil. Money itself is completely innocent of all charges.

I have stated and reiterated that information is the currency, the money of the coming century. That is the truth. And it is your first indication that money will come in many forms as we evolve. The biggest change between the twentieth century and the twenty-first century will come not in money but in the way we perceive money and how much we allow it to dictate our lives. Although important, money will not be the top item on the mission statement of the guerrilla entrepreneur. Enough money will be one goal, but more than enough money can get you in trouble.

Philosopher and psychologist Gregory Bateson said that humans must have balanced relationships with everything on earth. If we don't have enough magnesium in our systems, we will be in big trouble. If we have too much, it will be toxic to us. If we have the right amount, all will be well. The same thing is true for money. Not enough is a problem. Too much can be *Money can* toxic. The right amount to cover a person's needs is comfortable
be toxic and healthy. Guerrillas are not blinded by money and know when enough is enough. I am not saying that they are Spartan. No way. But I do want to plant the notion that money should be seen in its proper perspective. It is not the key to life. It is not the key to the universe.

This is not to say that enlightened businesses no longer list money as a major priority. Instead, cash is no longer the number one priority. It is not disdained, only reduced in rank. And it has changed in form as well. Not all of it can be folded.

Increasing numbers of workers in America are opting to take their money in the form of free time, healthier surroundings, better working conditions. They are settling for lower salaries in exchange for working fewer hours. They are choosing to be paid less money in return for living in a community with clean air, a more natural outdoor environment, and lower prices. They are selecting opportunity over income. Money is no longer the entire target, but part of the target.

Some money transactions will take the form of barter. Barter is one of the fastest-growing segments of the U.S. economy. In 1994, 55 percent of all the media purchased in America wasn't really purchased. It was bartered for. Just yesterday, I agreed to lower my fee to write a brochure for a concert producer in exchange for tickets to upcoming concerts.

Another form of money will be perks: tickets to ballgames and special events, memberships in clubs, use of a company vacation house, automobiles, education for kids, cruises and flights to meetings in exotic locales, access to company airplanes—the list is as long as your imagination is vivid. These perks will substitute for money.

Take me out to the ballgame

The next century will provide perks unknown to us right now—free online hours for your family, adventure trips with your work associates, technological pleasures and treasures from the realm of science fiction. We have entered that world already.

Money will change as much as the incentives it purchases. Right now, you are familiar with money and checks and credit cards and debit cards. Are you aware of e-cash? Cybercash? Digicash? These are but a few of the names for *electronic money* that flows through channels outside the banking system—and it moves more economically, conveniently, and quickly than foldable money. This kind of currency already exists in the burgeoning commerce on the Internet.

As I write this, Microsoft, Xerox, Visa, and Citicorp are creating infrastructures for electronic money. It's part of our evolution. Seashells were probably the first form of money used by humankind, followed by animal skins, rough-hewn coins, and then gold and silver. These succumbed to paper money, and now look what's happening—your wad of cash is being replaced by electronic bits.

Soon, you'll be able to download your e-cash from your bank or another provider, allowing you to shop online. Stores, restaurants, taxis, and businesses of all kinds in your community will soon also gladly take e-cash. Your e-cash card will help make the transaction. And you'll be taking part in the biggest currency revolution since gold.

This is not something that may or may not happen. An online expert said, "The genie's out of the bottle. The Internet doesn't have an off switch." You can be sure that guerrilla entrepreneurs are comfortable breathing the alien air of the Internet and benefiting from the cybercurrency revolution. They know that they *must* become familiar with e-cash because their customers will be familiar with it. That's why it's happening so rapidly in the first place.

Money is undergoing a high-speed transformation as speed and convenience are sought by society. Already, some people never carry money, considering it the effluvia of existence rather than honoring it. We also will treat it with less honor; most people will carry symbols of it, such as checks or cards, but few will carry the cash itself.

As a guerrilla entrepreneur, you will find that money is the most emotionally charged business issue. You will also witness a relaxation of the emotional connection with money, the attitude that spawns greed.

Money triggers a unique behavioral response in most individuals. This response is not rooted in the more civilized parts of our brain, where rationality reigns, but comes from a more primitive part, where there is no room for sanity or sense. The response is actually instinctive, part of a survival mechanism.

Columbia University conducted a study of people's behavior concerning money. They set up hidden cameras in banks and then observed the videotapes. They noticed that smiling people stopped smiling the moment they entered a bank. Animated and extroverted people stopped gesturing and became more introverted when they came within the confines of a bank. Panning around the faces, observers could see a noticeable absence of smiles, a definite presence of grimness. The study showed that people are more solemn in a bank than they are in church.

Might this study demonstrate a worship of money? A deep-seated feeling that money is holy? Or does it indicate a sense of smallness when compared with the wealth of a bank? It probably confirms all of these things.

Fortunately, although money is still necessary for survival, it is not part of our DNA; with the increasing desire for other types of success, it will become less of a motivator of human behavior.

The guerrilla entrepreneur is a person in business, a person devoted to earning profits, a person involved with matters that connect, directly or indirectly, with money. He is not emotionally connected to money, but he realizes that his prospects and his customers do not share this attitude. Most of them are still emotionally tied up with m-o-n-e-y, and he'll have to remember that when dealing with them.

This means that many customers will be wooed by offers to lower prices, save money, increase their income. The strong emotional connection to money will also manifest itself to you as a guerrilla entrepreneur whenever you try to collect money that is owed to you. Do they owe you the money? Yes. Will they pay you? Maybe. Maybe? Why only maybe?

Will they pay you? Maybe.

Again, it's because of the undeniable magnetism of money. People do not want to part with it, no matter how much they have. They can't help themselves. It is still part of *their* emotional makeup, even if it is not part of yours. Your job as a guerrilla is to get your just rewards. Be sure you not only get an agreement on money in writing, which decreases your potential encounter with litigation (and time spent litigating for money is time subtracted from your stay in heaven) but also get the money *in advance.* You can get it in advance with credit cards, debit cards, and cybercash. You may be forced, as a sane business practice, to get cash up front in all business transactions. The less you rely on the old form of money, the easier it will be to get your just rewards. People will not be able to pay you late in order to hold on to their own cash for the maximum amount of time. I would rather be paid $10 for a book than bill somebody $20 for the same book.

The guerrilla entrepreneur understands the psychology of money, has an enlightened view of it, and realizes that her customers do not. The last thing an entrepreneur wants to do is devote time and energy toward *collecting* money. Being a success should not involve doing any unnecessary work, and col-

How to avoid collecting

lecting money that should have been paid is unnecessary work.

Obtaining money is indeed necessary. But guerrillas structure their business so that they need not dedicate themselves to getting what is theirs. If they don't charge everything in advance, they charge half their fee or cost in advance. Or they get paid automatically upon delivery. Or credit cards and debit cards remove the collection task from their lives. Or their customers are so trusted that collection is never a problem.

I warn you of this because I know of more than a few entrepreneurs who did everything right in the creation, organization, and operation of their businesses. But when it came time to collect the money they had earned—it was no go. They had to devote many hours to collecting, wasting the energy that they should have put into drumming up business. They had to hire a collection agency and settle for only a portion of what they were owed. These good people had done their homework, were completely honest, and lived up to the promises they made. But they ultimately grew to dislike their businesses intensely—and only because collection of money was so difficult.

Credit cards are in greater use than ever before. Companies happily arrange to deduct their bills from customers' checking accounts. Bills are automatically paid by banks each month. The reason is convenience, to be sure, but also certainty that the bill will be paid on time, that the company will not have to do the dirty task of collecting. This convenience and certainty will be hallmarks of dealing with money in the coming millennium.

Although a tight economy requires that people save money as much as possible, and in spite of the enormous growth of huge discount warehouse retail operations, all guerrilla entrepreneurs have learned that price is not the primary sales claim upon which to build a lasting success.

People who select a business to patronize strictly based upon low price are the worst kind of customers—disloyal and easily taken away by others offering even lower prices. Loyal customers are nine times more profitable to a business than disloyal customers. One study reported in *Advertising Age* revealed that price was only the fifth most important reason to patronize a business. More important than price were selection, service, quality, and confidence in the business. In a nutshell, value will always be regarded as more important than price. Of every product category in the United States, from automobiles to toothpaste, from shoes to beer, the leader of each category is *never* the product with the lowest price. Leaders offer benefits of all kinds, but the lowest price is not one of them. And it does not have to be.

The study I just referred to reported that only 13 percent of Americans list price as the most important factor influencing a purchase. That means that 87 percent of us now comprehend that there are considerations more significant than money.

Guerrilla entrepreneurs realize that money fits into their grand scheme of generosity. They know well the words of the poet Carl Sandburg, "Money is like manure—good only when spread around." And beneath it all, at their *own* bottom line, they are aware of the truth of the words of the economist who said, "Solvency is entirely a matter of temperament and not of income." Guerrillas have an evolved temperament in matters of money. Their yardsticks are beyond the financial ones.

"Money is like manure"

PART II

The Setting

THINK OF YOURSELF as a guerrilla entrepreneur working either from a special room in your home, a room brimming with all the working technology you'll need, or from an office space peopled with comfortably clad coworkers, far more efficient yet less formal than the office space of the past.

Perhaps the setting for your work is a high-rise building smack-dab in the middle of town. Maybe it's on an island in the middle of a lake at the edge of a large city. Possibly it's in an office area above the residential area in the building where you live. Or it's on a boat heading for Fiji, of all places, and there you are, communicating by using satellites, your modem, and your trusty computer.

As a guerrilla entrepreneur, the setting for your work will be of your own choosing. The best things about your setting will be the things you have in it: your technological stuff to save your time and energy, and the people with whom you work. They seem to be on your wavelength more than people in the past. Guerrilla companies have a way of attracting guerrilla-minded people.

If you are still forced to travel to work, your commute will allow you to achieve your goals, whatever they may be, for the commuter vehicles of the future will blend safety with efficiency, providing drivers and passengers with options other than driving. Although the world will be highly efficient, the stress of working in it will be noticeably lower because of the burden taken up by technology.

The life of a guerrilla entrepreneur will provide you with an optimum blend of the old—valued coworkers, leisure time, opportunities to be with your family, and the new—evolved communications, a link to the Internet, and a computer that will save you loads of time. It will place you where you want to be, not where your boss says you should be. And it will enable you to awaken each morning looking forward to your workday, rather than dreading it.

If this sounds a bit as if you are living in your own dream, you are seeing clearly the way of the guerrilla.

9

Business in the New Millennium

YOU CAN BE sure of two things in the twenty-first century: business will be a lot harder, and business will be a lot easier.

It will be harder because of five factors:

1. Time

Time will become magnified in importance. The luxury of spare time at work is a luxury of the past. Spare time will be revered, but not at work. You will notice that almost everyone will share the new awareness of time. Customers will demand and expect speed. You will, too.

2. Contact

Less face-to-face contact will remove much of the social warmth of working. People now get over half their messages by other forms of communication, such as answering machines, e-mail, and fax machines. Such communications can be misunderstood or inaccurate; verbal accuracy will grow in value. The joy of social interaction will be diminished.

3. Change

Change will be thrust upon us, and much that we counted on before will no longer hold forth. Even things we learn will be true only for a short time before being surpassed by new truths. Genius will not consist of learning something, but in learning one thing after another. If you can't adapt, you aren't cut out to be a guerrilla.

4. Talent

Talent will become diffuse as top people trade the vitality of a huge corporation for the tranquillity of working at home. Well and good for them, but for guerrilla entrepreneurs, this means all the big brains won't be under one roof. You'll have to scout them out.

5. Technology

Technology will be more important in your life, and you'll have to understand it to take full advantage of it. But technology is becoming easier to use, user manuals are written more clearly, and the nature of training (repetition will be your friend for life) has improved. If you're technophobic, see a technoshrink.

The ways business will be easier

There are really five thousand ways in which business will be easier in the next millennium, but for purposes of time and space, let's just discuss five here:

1. Time

You will have more time to do what really must be done, rather than wasting time with busywork, because of technological advancements. Your network of independent contractors will also free up more of your time. Use it to increase your profits, to make your business better, or to just plain enjoy yourself.

2. Values

Values will change, and they will be more in keeping with your own guerrilla values. In the twentieth century, the main value was making money. In the twenty-first century, that priority will take a back seat to the human values of happiness at work, free time, family, spirituality. As you are discovering, profit seeking will never be eliminated, only reprioritized.

3. Advancements

New advancements in business, both psychological and technological, will make the workplace more exciting, easier to use, even enjoyable. Flextime and teleconferencing will make for less crowded commuting, if you commute at all. The virtual office is the at-home office.

4. Procedures

Streamlined procedures will keep your work life efficient, organized, simple, and fast. You won't waste time or effort at work because you'll have learned to become an efficient working machine, and, as a guerrilla entrepreneur, you'll realize that the whole purpose of streamlining is to add *effectiveness*.

5. People

You will deal with smarter but fewer people. Your workplace won't be populated with paper-shufflers. Your at-home business will put you into contact with bright, talented entrepreneurs who made the break from the corporate life and are doing very well, just like you.

Yet even with all the changes, positive and negative, business in the new millennium will be one millennium tougher than it used to be because of greater complexity, tougher competition and more of it, better information, more enlightened people, more educated players, new technology, changes whizzing by faster than ever before.

Does that mean that everything is changing and everything is going to be new? It does not, though some people will fall into the fool's pit of thinking all the rules have changed. Five fundamental things will not change, and although they may change *What won't* in the far distant future, the rate of their change will be so slow *change* that you'll be better off thinking of them as nearly static:

1. Human Nature

People will be people, with the usual strengths and foibles. They will be creatures of their emotions even though their brains will have evolved, and they will still want to be treated fairly and kindly.

2. Wants, Needs, and Fears

People will continue to want and need love and security, money and power, a sense of identity, a feeling of well-being. They will fear the same things they fear now: lack of control, illness, absence of love and security.

3. Youth and Age

They'll be just as they are now: young people will still be the first to try new things, and old people will still control most of the wealth. The generation gap will never close, but it will move. Every child will still grow up to be either like their parents or a reaction to their parents.

4. Spirituality

Although people will differ in where they turn to find a higher power, they will continue to seek it and continue to find it. Spirituality will continue to motivate the best that is within people. There will be a renaissance as people recognize their own inherent spirituality. It has already started.

5. Problems

Entrepreneurs who can solve them will be sought-after members of society. Even in a smokeless society, where nobody is trying to quit smoking, zillions will still be trying to earn more money, lose weight, attract the opposite sex, make friends, and break bad habits, whatever those habits may be—from addiction to the Internet to addiction to work.

Business in the new millennium is going to be extremely challenging, just the ticket for guerrilla entrepreneurs who are not smothered by tradition and who are open to new opportunities. *How to be lucky* You will be among the lucky ones if you realize that luck is what you get when you combine *preparation* with *opportunity*.

Guerrillas will be lucky because they did their homework, researched their opportunities, got the training they required, and opened their minds to the new century. This is the *preparation* demanded by the twenty-first century. The *opportunity* comes in putting out the word on what you do, connecting with fellow guerrillas, being a presence in the online world, having the commitment to stick with your plan—and having a plan in the first place.

When preparation meets opportunity, the world will view you as a very lucky person. But in reality, you took charge of your luck. You made it happen. There was nothing accidental about it.

Bill Gates, cofounder and CEO of Microsoft, studied enough to know how to develop a new computer technology. Then he researched the computer community to spot vulnerabilities. He found one—complex computer operating systems—and then set about solving the problem in his own guerrilla way. His company has made him one of the wealthiest Americans on the planet. Gosh, he was lucky!

Business people in the twenty-first century will surely be fed up with the promise of new developments on the technical horizon. They will have learned, often by expensive and painful lessons, that many new developments won't happen for another fifty years and others will never happen at all. Some other innovation will come down the pike, making the promised technology obsolete before it even flies, such as the rapid growth of computerized graphics making high-definition television obsolete before it ever had a chance to flourish in America.

Guerrilla entrepreneurs won't let their eyes glaze over at the promise of new technology. They will be involved with "here and now" developments more than "distant horizon" developments. They have the patience to wait; they realize that today's technology can propel them to their goals without waiting for somebody's hare-brained (alas, it's often the case) scheme to get off the drawing board.

Here and now

While some business owners were waiting for computer technology to drop in price, others were making a fortune with the higher-priced older computers. When the new ones were introduced—and debugged—the guerrillas had made so much money that they didn't care much about the savings then available.

In the new millennium, business will be conducted everywhere—at comfortable homes, high-tech offices, sports arena luxury boxes, tropical beaches; on airplanes, in cars, in in-person meetings, by fax on cruise liners.

Increasingly, information will come by way of the Internet. Business schools will be forced to update their curricula; their case histories from the past will no longer be relevant in a society that has left the past behind. Maybe the past used to be the key to the future. In the coming century, it will be the key to disaster. New rules, new ways of working, new places to work, new factors influencing a decision, and an entirely new marketplace will make change a necessity.

Two guerrilla musts   The past did not list computer literacy or typing ability as skills of a business leader. The present proves that they are musts. The past did not require that you know a second or third language, that you deal gracefully with people from other cultures. The past did not ask you to be interactive, but the future demands it. The Nintendo champ of the year? He used to be a novelty. Now he's the chairman of the board of a Fortune 500 company.

The majority of the esteemed members of the 1980 Fortune 500 list compiled by *Fortune* magazine are no longer with us—having become extinct through mergers, acquisitions, bankruptcies, new technology, and inability to keep up with change.

If those companies hadn't warbled their swan songs in the 1980s and 1990s, you would be hearing their mournful tunes in the twenty-first century, when change will happen faster than ever and casualties will drop by the wayside at a record pace. Although on the surface it looks as though faceless corporations bit the dust during the downsizing mania of the late twentieth century, the reality is that *people* were biting the dust: families with kids and hopes for the future. Guerrilla entrepreneurs will never fall prey to such ugliness during an economic downturn.

They will have disaster plans built into their success plan. They know the inevitability of change. Only those not prepared for it do the suffering.

E. F. Schumacher, who wrote *Small Is Beautiful,* might have been the first to coin the phrase, but the sentiment is lived by guerrillas now more than ever. Guerrillas understand the acute need for downsizing, not as it was meant in the twentieth century, but the way guerrillas will mean it in the twenty-first.

If you are irrevocably bound to the notion of making your company grow large, you're going to have to make it small first. Guerrillas may have the goal of market domination, but to achieve it, they must first implement *selective shrinking.* Guerrillas view the following dozen areas with an eye toward shrinking them over time. Some of these areas should start out small and stay that way. Others should be reduced slowly over time.

Selective shrinking

1. Downsize Your Marketing Weapon Arsenal

The process of guerrilla marketing calls for you to examine and then select a large variety of marketing weapons. Before launching them, you should put them into priority order; then fire them in slow motion. Guerrilla marketing attacks should not be sudden. There's rarely a need to rush. Carefully keep track of which weapons are hitting bull's-eyes and which are missing the target. Eliminate the loser techniques. Double up on the winners. The idea is to end up with a small, lethal selection of weapons, every one proved in action.

2. Downsize Your Categories of Prospects

Guerrillas know well the need to test, and so test they do — messages, media, prices, prospects, and a whole lot more. They test a wide range of prospects, using direct marketing and mass marketing. This lets them know which prospects to ignore from now on and which to concentrate upon. Unless they check out a comprehensive selection of prospects, they may miss out on the hottest of all. They want to market like crazy, but *only* to their most torrid prospects. Guerrillas have A-lists, identifying their most rewarding prospects and customers, and they have B-lists, containing the names of those prospects and customers who are less than prime. They focus primarily on that A-list and never hesitate to play favorites.

3. Downsize the Number of Departments in Your Business

If your marketing department is separate from your sales department, there's a chance they'll be marching to different tunes and out of step with each other. This is true of all departments. They don't act as cohesively as you'd like; each functions more as a single department than as part of a whole business. The more they are merged, the more they will understand the common goal and help one another. Simplicity was, is, and will be the byword. Ancient wisdom still holds true: "In the beginner's mind there are many possibilities, but in the expert's mind there are few."

4. Downsize the Number of Key People in Your Company

Business is not a democracy, and although the guerrilla is fast to delegate, rarely doing anything herself that can be delegated, the guerrilla does not delegate ultimate authority. A business is usually as good as the weakest member of top management. The meaning is clear: only your best should be at the top. You may have many who are good, but very few who are the best.

5. Downsize Your Mission Statement

A narrow focus will be your ally when you create or update your statement of purpose. You did not create your company to do all things for all people, but to do some things for some people with excellence. Employees, customers, prospects, and suppliers should be tuned in to a mission they understand and can help you accomplish.

6. *Downsize Your Focus*

You may have inaugurated your business with a wide focus, but as you become more experienced and, we hope, wiser, you can adjust that focus and make it smaller. The more acute the focus, the better equipped you will be to succeed, for you will be able to increase your effectiveness and decrease the amount of money used in the past to reach a large target.

7. *Downsize Your Niche*

The more specialized your niche, the easier it will be to establish it, communicate it, and live up to it. Now that you've been around for a while, perhaps you realize that your old niche was too broad. If you can fill a need that no one else fills, occupy a position that is yours alone, your path to success will be smoother.

8. *Downsize Your Marketing Plan*

The purpose of your marketing may be clearer to you now, and your plan can reflect your enlightenment. The best benefits for you to emphasize are also better known to you now than they were at day one. Your target audiences should be smaller in number, your weaponry more selective. Even your budget can be downsized because you have learned which weapons and tactics to eliminate.

9. *Downsize Your Ad Size and Commercial Length*

You don't need the impact of large ads as much as the consistency of smaller ads after you've established your business. In ten seconds of TV time, you can tell a story that used to take thirty seconds. Your one-minute radio spots can be half that length now. Nearly 80 percent of national TV spots are under thirty seconds in length these days, and it's not the new guys who have that luxury. It's the guerrillas among the behemoths.

10. Downsize the World

That global village you've been hearing about all these years? It's here now. Planet earth has been shrunk by the Internet far more than by the Concorde, making it more manageable, easier to market to, not as intimidating. To do business internationally, you need a mouse instead of a passport. As of this moment, 154 nations are connected to the Internet, and you can visit any one of them on your computer monitor. No more jet lag.

11. Downsize the Number of Your Competitors

As you become smarter and conduct your business more effectively, you will save marketing funds while wreaking havoc among your competition. Few will be able to stand up to the withering effects of your guerrilla marketing attack. You will have paid the dues of failed experiments and will then reap the benefits of a selective arsenal of weapons. No wonder the competition will fall by the wayside.

12. Downsize the Number of Hours You Are Working

From the start, when you launch your guerrilla enterprise, and later on, when it is running smoothly and profitably, make sure there is balance in your life. You'll probably end up having more energy to devote to your business and a better perspective if you pull back a bit and become involved in something other than your work. It is true that work is noble, but so are you—and you're here on earth to do more than work hard.

Now that you know about downsizing many elements of your business, exactly what are you going to do about it? I know that you have absorbed what you have just read, but will you act upon it?

One-way brains and two-way brains

People have either *one-way brains* or *two-way brains*. People with one-way brains learn what they are taught. From books, tapes, seminars, and other sources, they comprehend their lessons, but never act upon what they have learned. People with two-way brains absorb and then act upon their new knowledge.

Guerrillas downsize for success. Now that you've seen business from their perspective, study your own response to it, and see if you have a one-way brain or a two-way brain.

Two-way brains are standard operational guerrilla equipment for the future. Success at business in the twenty-first century depends upon your having that particular equipment. A brain that can do only half the tasks demanded of it will get you into a lot of trouble if you're to be an entrepreneur. The way of the guerrilla requires that you *take action* to give wings to your wisdom.

10

The Omnipotence
of Tiny Details

A COMPANY can market well, service with grace, offer exceptional values, and still fall flat on its face. That company may have done the big and important things very well, but neglected tiny details. *Flash:* Those tiny details are as important as the primary thrust of the business. What do you think is the prime factor determining a woman's selection of where she buys her gasoline? Power? Service? Price? It's the *bathroom.* A tiny detail for a multi-billion-dollar oil company, right? Wrong. *Not* a tiny detail, except to a tiny mind.

All of us do business with companies and individuals based upon their ability to recognize and attend to tiny details. Ten examples from my life, five with small companies, five with huge ones, cast more light on this:

1. Don Collins Buick has been getting my business since 1971 because of details. They drive me home while my car is being serviced and then pick me up. They wash my car, whether or not I ask for it. They service a minor part, tell me about it, but charge nothing. My final price is always less than their estimate. They always have my car ready ahead of schedule. They scour the state to help me get parts. They've helped keep my car alive from new until now, when I have a third of a million miles on it. And I like the fact that the service manager wears a tie.

2. John Wathen of Fearless Computing has been my computer consultant/retailer/technician since I received his first postcard mailing—offering a free cleaning of my computer—in 1988. Since then, I've purchased several computers and associ-

ated peripherals from him, had all installed and serviced by him, got my software from him, tapped his telephone trouble-shooting talents, and leaned on him for every single computer problem and opportunity—without leaving home. His house calls and attentiveness to the smallest detail have endeared him to me forever. Plus, he gets better computer prices for me than I could ever get for myself. And the name of his company makes me believe he's up to tackling *any* computer problem.

House calls

3. Celina Aquilar has been our housecleaner for only a few months now. But she's the only cleaning lady we've had in forty years who folds my T-shirts so that the words on them are showing and then puts them in alphabetical order on a high shelf in my closet. The rest of her cleaning is even more meticulous.

4. Every waiter and waitress at Kamikaze Restaurant knows my wife's and my favorite table, that my wife wants a Coke and a fork, that I want water and chopsticks plus an extra napkin, and that we both want teriyaki sauce on our rice. Each time we eat dinner there, we are asked about our daughter. Insignificant details, right? Wrong. Significant details. How are the food and the prices? They're the same as everyone else's—except in the detail department.

5. I once helped a company, IFS, market their services. They help schools raise funds. At the completion of a project, they used to send a bill asking for their half of the proceeds from the sale, leaving the school with the other half. Their bills were worded something like this: "Balance due: $5,200." Schools would pay, but slowly. Then IFS changed the wording on the bill to this: "Congratulations! Your school earned $5,200! Now, please pay our balance of $5,200." This tiny detail sped up their collections dramatically.

6. Visa, MasterCard, American Express—they were all the same to me. Not Discover, mind you. I would *never* use a Discover card for reasons I'll disclose in the next example. Suddenly, I began to use Visa and only Visa. Why? Simply because they hooked up with United Airlines, and I realized that I could start flying for free. I know that other credit cards have since

connected with other airlines, but Visa did it first. And Visa still gets my business.

7. At Sears, I used to buy as much as I possibly could buy in every single department—from tools to toys, from gardening to automotive needs. Then I was late paying a bill. The next month, I needed new tires. Because I had been a fast-paying charge customer at Sears for over ten years, I figured I could easily put the tires on my charge account, only one month *Sears wouldn't* overdue. "Cash or no tires," I was told. "And we won't take a *take my check* check." You can see their point. You can also see mine. I bought my tires at Don Collins Buick and never have made a purchase from Sears since, and I disdain the Discover card forever because it's from Sears.

8. Federal Express delivers to some of the tallest skyscraper office buildings in the world and to some of the largest corporations. It also delivers to my house, down my steep driveway, and puts my packages, when I'm not around, into a cooler I keep outside to hold tennis balls for my dog. When I'm home, I see the driver give a dog biscuit to my dog! My packages don't always absolutely, positively have to get anywhere the next day. But my dog sure loves the sight of that Federal Express delivery van. That silly detail influences my choice of delivery services. Maybe it's not so silly after all.

9. Walt Disney sure had it right with his penchant for cleanliness. His ability to recognize that neatness is *not a detail* is one of the reasons for the success of Disneyland and other Disney parks. Their management and staff treat neatness as a goal and a benefit, knowing that neat premises suggest a neatly run company—just as sloppy premises do the opposite. Guerrillas realize that neatness is a marketing weapon, a little detail that costs nothing but the right attitude.

10. Taco Bell has a location just minutes from where I live. One day several years ago, my wife and I were not only hungry, but hungry for Mexican food. In fact, we were hungry for Taco Bell's version of Mexican food. We wanted to eat in the restaurant, one of the nicer Taco Bells we'd seen. It looked spotless

inside. Disney would have approved. As we looked over the menu, we noticed an ultrapowerful aroma of ammonia cleaner in the restaurant. The people who had cleaned the premises understood the concept of cleanliness but not the concept that a restaurant should smell like delicious food. The smell was so overpowering that all thoughts of Taco Bell, Mexican food, and eating disappeared. Instead of ordering, my wife and I hightailed it out of there and into the fresh clear air. We rolled down the windows, though there was no trace of the smell in the car, as we drove to another restaurant where we could count on the aromas of Indian food. The memory of aromas has a remarkably long life span. I suppose that's why we've never been back to a Taco Bell. *Tacos and ammonia cleaner*

The guerrilla entrepreneur makes a details list for her enterprise. The list spells out the details that affect her business connections: how the phone is answered, the neatness of the premises, the sincerity of her customer follow-up, the extra things she does that give the perception of value at no cost. The way that Don Collins Buick provides transportation for me certainly does that. That little dog biscuit that the Federal Express driver gives away can't be the *only* one *any* driver gives away. There must be lots of doggie lovers grateful for this extra value. *A details list*

A guerrilla details list needs to take the senses into account:

* Sight—signage, brightness, clarity, color, typeface, readability
* Sound—music, loudness or softness, opportunity for silence
* Smell—old or new, clean or dirty, appetizing or off-putting
* Touch—rough or smooth, cheap or expensive, pleasant, solid
* Taste—probably applicable only to food and drink guerrillas

A details list also goes beyond those Aristotelian senses into the senses of wonder, humor, expectancy, history, health, well-being, security, honesty, and efficiency. You tell the dry cleaner, "It's important that you button these particular buttons on my button-down shirt." Each time, the dry cleaner overlooks the small detail, which is not a small detail to you, or you wouldn't have asked. So it's no surprise when you switch dry cleaners.

Tiny details that can undo large efforts exist in any business. Of course, they include customer service, where details abound, and guerrillas strike gold by attending to details overlooked by the less prepared. Guerrillas are aware of the need to save time, so they orient what they do to save time for their customers and clients. Minor details. Major payoffs.

Ten details that will help or hurt you

Beyond service, which is obvious, guerrilla entrepreneurs have discovered that details can help or hurt you in these ten areas:

1. Telephone

How your telephone is answered and what happens when the person is on hold influence that person's opinion of your business. Guerrillas *actively train* anyone who will answer the phone, knowing it is a lifeline to business and that only very special people call. When callers are put on hold, they should hear a recording that gives fascinating information that may prove valuable to them.

2. Business Card

What your business card says, what it looks like, and what makes it keepable can make the difference between a customer's occasional patronization and frequent purchases. Business cards have changed. Guerrilla entrepreneurs give away cards that not only have their address, phone and fax numbers, and e-mail address, but also open up to provide information about their offerings, services, and benefits.

3. Business Hours

The hours and days you are open and the methods of getting in touch with you make your business either convenient or inconvenient. People expect to be able to contact you when it is *convenient for them*. They want to hook up with your voice mail or e-mail or fax machine or pager or something, and they don't want to wait. Easy to contact means easy to buy from.

4. Community Work

The time and hard work that you put *into the community* on an unpaid basis can have a dramatic impact on your business. You might not expect coaching a Little League team to be a business tactic, but your business is part of your life. By giving something to the community, you open wide the conduits through which good things flow into and out of your life.

5. Cleanliness

The tidiness of your premises, inside and out, especially the restrooms, is noticed by more people than you may imagine. You might be a bit shocked to know how many people are so put off by messiness that it will keep them forever away from the mess. They really will believe that the messiness pervades your entire organization. Luckily, guerrillas know neatness counts.

6. Customer Appreciation

The ability of your salespeople to make customers and prospects feel unique can make the difference between getting one-time customers and all-the-time customers. It is easy for me to tell you this. It will be difficult for you to accomplish, but essential if survival, not to mention prosperity, is on your mind. Attention to detail is the key, and research is your guide to detail. Customers must feel that you know what they really are: one of a kind.   *One of a kind*

7. Philanthropy

Your company's involvement with a noble cause beyond mere profits will affect people's perception of your business and their desire to do business with you. Align your company with a social cause that will help the planet. Actively work for that cause, and contribute a share of your profits to it. Support organizations or activities that address the problems of the environment, the homeless, AIDS, multiple sclerosis—many causes need your help.

8. Memory

Don't forget how you feel when someone remembers your name or your business name. It proves that you mean something to them. It seems like a minor detail, but it happens so infrequently that it's a major detail.

9. Flexibility

A detail everyone will remember, possibly even talk about, is how you *veer from your usual practices* and render special service. A Nordstrom department store couldn't deliver a dress to my wife on time, so the salesman offered to deliver it himself. My wife still talks about it, still buys from Nordstrom.

10. Promotional Freebies

Freebies are always appreciated by all demographic groups, all age groups, all income groups. People expect to pay for things and do not expect to get anything for free. They will long remember your generosity and certainly will remember your name.

A customer of your competitor

By far the best way to become a guerrilla master of details is to become a customer of yourself and a customer of your competitor. See how you, or a stand-in for you, is treated by each business—especially in the details. Become a customer of more competitors, especially the leaders, and study intensely the details of how they handle their businesses. Visit them. Shop them. Browse with them. Consult with them. Are they attending to any details overlooked by you?

Are there any details that nobody attends to—ones that you might handle in a way that separates you from the crowd? To be a guerrilla entrepreneur, you must realize that in the relationship between a business and its customers, there is no such thing as an unimportant or minor detail.

11

Warm Relationships with Customers

WE SHOULD LEARN from an old proverb: "If you want to be prosperous for a year, grow grain. If you want to be prosperous for ten years, grow trees. If you want to be prosperous for a lifetime, grow people." To be an effective guerrilla entrepreneur, you'll have to grow your business through every person you come into contact with — employees, associates, and customers.

Your customers can be transformed into dynamite salespeople, giving you the joy of repeat sales by selling to themselves, and giving you the economy and bliss of referral sales by selling to others. All it takes is a caring, cozy, warm relationship with your customers. It is much easier to have warm relationships than cool relationships. Cool relationships aren't much fun, so you won't *want* to nurture them as much as you will warm relationships. Warm relationships are close, personal, and caring, with lots of contact and follow-up. Cool relationships are all business. Many guerrillas have learned that the warm relationships are often the best part of running the business.

As a guerrilla entrepreneur, you must appreciate the underlying truth about what business you are in. Whether you're in the book business, welding business, software business, or delivery business, you also are in the *people* business, and the more energetically you nod your head while reading this, the better you are at running your business. Guerrilla marketers know that warm relationships

The people business

* Come from *consistent follow-up*
* Come from *knowing the customer's name*

* Come from *giving more than is expected*
* Come from *eye contact and smiles*
* Come from *asking and listening alertly*
* Come *individually and not in groups*
* Involve *knowing personal data about people,* not merely business data
* Are created *through caring service*
* Come *when everyone wants them*
* Form the *foundation for future prosperity*

* * *

The days of thinking about sales are days of a soon-to-be-bygone century. Modern thinking is centered around *relationships*—human-to-human contacts—whenever possible. These come in greatest profusion to those who understand that they are fundamentally in the people business.

Become an expert

How do you go into the people business? Easy. You become an expert on your own customers. Know what makes them tick, what makes them love you, what makes them buy your products or services. Harvey Mackay, author of *Swim with the Sharks Without Being Eaten Alive*, said, "Knowing something about your customer is just as important as knowing everything about your product."

Mackay knows so much about his customers that when holiday time rolls around, his company, the Mackay Envelope Company, *never* sends corporate Christmas cards. "Anyone can send a corporate Christmas card," he says, "but nobody ever says, 'Hey, thanks for the corporate Christmas card.'" Instead, his company sends Thanksgiving Day cards. Nobody else sends them, so they are noticed by all who receive them. Best of all, though, is what he says on the card. It's not merely "Happy Thanksgiving," because anybody could say that. Mackay's Thanksgiving Day cards say something personal, such as "Happy Thanksgiving, and congratulations on your daughter's making the cheerleader squad!" That's the sign of a warm relationship, a relationship that is going to get closer and stronger.

By the way, Mackay says that over 70 percent of the cards he sends elicit a thank-you.

We are now in the middle of an era of intense competition—one in which satisfying and delighting the customer is crucial not only to business success, but even to business survival. Guerrilla entrepreneurs have the knack of creating intimacy between themselves and their customers. This intimacy comes not only when you ask many questions (the key that opens the lock to information), but also when the customer becomes aware of how carefully you listen to the answers.

Creating *intimacy* is a talent that must be mastered by you and by everyone who interacts with customers for you. The warm relationships guerrillas seek exist not only between one person and the customer, but between many of your people and the customer. The service you provide must be part of your company's very makeup. It must not only look like, but actually *be* second nature to you. And this will happen if you realize the importance of a warm relationship and if you actually enjoy it. Caring and giving must become a *habit* within your company. *How to be intimate*

More and more, the idea that marketing *originates at the sale* makes sense. Guerrillas thrive on this concept because they realize that nearly 70 percent of customer loss occurs due to apathy after the sale, and so they never allow apathy to set in. They also know that over 70 percent of customer defections from a business have absolutely nothing to do with the product. So they work like crazy to establish a close tie with customers, a tie that becomes even stronger after the sale has been made.

Guerrilla entrepreneurs create immediate and lasting rapport with prospects, customers, and clients. They know well that people buy from people they like and trust. These same guerrillas search out qualified prospects who can become long-term clients. Then they maintain those client relationships in a mutually profitable way. This leads to referral and repeat business, which is very profitable and saves costly prospecting time.

To make your relationship as powerful as possible, find out as much as possible about each customer so that you can tailor your service to that customer's needs. A bookstore had a database that showed that a customer frequently purchased books about the airline industry, so the bookstore mailed a short, warm note to that customer after receiving three new books about the industry. The customer *knew* he was not part of a mass mailing, and whether he bought the new books or not, *remembered* that this bookstore rendered service that was out of the ordinary.

A liquor store owner called a customer, informing her that he had just purchased several cases of a particular 1989 cabernet sauvignon from the Alexander Valley in Sonoma County, California, and that he knew how much the customer loved wines from that specific valley. The store owner told the customer that he could let her have the wine at $6 per bottle. The customer, knowing the value she had been offered, was wildly appreciative of the phone call (how many calls like that have *you* received?) and not only bought a couple of cases of wine, but told the friends to whom she served it about how she came to buy it. Chalk up one more point for the guerrilla liquor store owner.

Five basic truths

The world-class renderer of service lives by five basic truths about customer relationships and how to keep them warm and comfortable:

1. *Make the customer feel unique.* If you do this, you will have established a serious competitive edge over all who would hope to woo your customer from you. If you can make a customer realize that you know what makes him or her unique, you have the potential for a lifetime relationship.

2. *Make the customer feel singled out.* When a customer knows that you have made not a mass-market offer, but a one-of-a-kind offer tailored specifically for the customer, you have struck it rich in your quest for a warm relationship.

3. *Make the customer feel that you want to be of service.* Many companies serve their customers well enough, but seem to be going through the motions. Guerrillas see to it that their employees want to help, honestly care, and render such good service that the customer can actually see they are happy to do so.

4. *Make sure you stay in constant touch with the customer.* The fancy word for this is follow-up, and guerrillas worship at its altar. They stay in touch with customers by phone and mail, with newsletters and direct mail letters. They use their follow-up to make sales, announce discounts, introduce new items, ask questions via all-important questionnaires, and ask for the names of potential new customers. This follow-up pays for itself while providing the added bonus of warming up the relationship through contact.

5. *Make sure you exceed the customer's expectations.* Guerrillas are generous, as you have undoubtedly learned, because they see the business rewards of giving. Their generosity also pays off in profits because by giving customers more than they bargained for, the guerrilla wins that customer's heart. Exceeding expectations is not the norm. If you exceed them, you will stand out. It is not easy to give that little extra, but try telling that to a guerrilla. You'll hear that what's really not easy is staying in business if you can't outperform all competitors.

In order to live by these five basic truths, you must have the soul of a guerrilla entrepreneur. You've got to have the *patience, passion, and persistence* of the person who is committed to success. Without these characteristics, it will be difficult to render the kind of service that twenty-first-century customers will demand and expect. Such service is remarkably rare right now, but as the competition heats up and customers gain sophistication, you will be forced, as the price of admission, to provide service that leads customers to want to make *your business* part of *their identity.* That's the payoff of a warm relationship.

You must also have *boundless energy*, because knocking yourself out for customers is just what you'll want to do, and you won't be able to do it unless you are fit physically and mentally. Others will wonder where you get your energy, but you'll know that it is generated by your passion for pleasing.

Never an energy crisis

Unless you have a *sense of responsibility*, you might be tempted to leave to others the rendering of warm service. That's great, if you can, but you've got to take the ultimate responsibility for the standards of your company's service, for the training of those who might represent you, and for the hiring or forging of alliances with these people.

To establish lasting relationships with customers, you must be *a stickler for detail*. Tiny, crucial details do not escape the notice of your customers; they must not be invisible to you. This is especially important in the beginning, when you are generating the momentum that results in superb service. Perhaps later, after the standards are clear to all, you can begin to delegate this vital chore.

You must have *decision-making ability* because rendering superior service often means making decisions on the spot. Nordstrom, one of the most honored retail chains in history when it comes to customer service, leaves virtually all service decisions to the salesperson. Unless that person is prepared to make a decision at the moment that a decision is needed, somebody is going to be dissatisfied. That's why Nordstrom *and* you must be prepared to decide such matters, despite the risk of being wrong. Guerrillas do not pale at the concept of failure.

One final entrepreneurial characteristic necessary to keep customers on your customer list is the *motivation to please*. Unless you are highly motivated to make your customers happy, you're just not going to be able to do it. In fact, if you lack this motivation, you might question whether or not you should be running your own business in the first place. Customers are the reason you are in business; you must aim to please them.

Why you're in business

There are lists of companies that render superlative service right now, and I could give you several pages of them. But that would be missing the point. Customer service and developing warm relationships are more a matter of common sense than anything else. I realize that common sense is more uncommon than ever before, but as a guerrilla, you should take that as an invitation to compete with confidence.

Your sensitivity to the needs of customers and your desire to please them will fuel your common sense so that you transform all first-time customers into lifetime customers. You'll do it because you want them to be happy, you never want them to defect to a competitor, and you realize the immense difference between a relationship that is a one-night stand and a relationship that is loving and lasting.

12

Close Relationships
with Suppliers

HENRY FORD once sued one of his suppliers for several million dollars. The company was a major supplier of nuts and bolts. The only basis of Ford's lawsuit was that the supplier had changed the dimensions of his wooden shipping cartons. He had been doing business with Ford for several years, satisfying the giant firm in every way, and so the supplier didn't think it would matter if the cartons were changed a tad.

Wrong. Ford won his lawsuit, proving that he had been using the flattened wooden shipping cartons as floorboards for his Ford motorcars, and showing that changing the dimensions severely hampered the Ford production line.

The guerrilla moral to the tale is that Ford had a relationship with his supplier that depended upon the right nuts and bolts being delivered to the right place at the right time, *plus* he received automotive structural materials at no cost, in the form of the shipping carton. Had his relationship been a close one rather than the impersonal bond he had created, Ford would have leveled with the supplier at the outset, showing how both of them could gain in the long run if the supplier stuck to the original container dimensions. Ford could have continued to save money if only he had offered to pay the supplier to ship in the same cartons instead of trying to get something for nothing.

Guerrilla entrepreneurs realize that their suppliers are more than mere providers of products or services. Suppliers can help guerrillas cut costs by shipping in containers of predetermined materials and dimensions. They can help guerrillas satisfy customers by keeping their promises about deliveries, knowing that if they foul up, it often makes the guerrilla look bad. They can help guerrillas save money by alerting them to any proposed price increases. They can clue guerrillas in on competitive activity, providing them with all-important reconnaissance, a perpetual guerrilla mission.

The savvy guerrilla entrepreneur views suppliers as *partners*, for that, in essence, is what they are. Each benefits from the actions of the other. Each profits from the excellence of the other. *Viewing suppliers as partners*

Once you realize that your supplier is actually your partner in the business process, you will want to learn more about that supplier, just as you continue learning about your own enterprise and about your customers. The closer you become to the supplier, the more you will gain a "favored nation" status. Old friends do favors for old friends.

To become close to your supplier, you must develop five modes of business behavior. *The care and feeding of suppliers*

1. Stay in Contact

Let your suppliers know when they've done something right as well as when they've done something wrong. Keep them up to date on your plans so that they can tailor their plans accordingly, and both of you will avoid crises.

2. Inform Suppliers of Your Marketing Plans

Give them advance notice so that they can be prepared for an influx of orders. This also lets them know how important you are in the industry and the community so that they will treat your company with the respect it deserves.

3. Be Loyal to Your Suppliers

Of course, you will always listen to competitive bids for your business, but deep down, you know that the best relationships are the old relationships, so you see it as your job to improve the supplier's prices, quality, service, or selection with your suggestions rather than deserting him for another. Get suppliers to know your company inside and out so that they develop radar for your needs.

4. Alert Your Supplier to Problems

Let your supplier know if you have a problem. Guerrillas do not harbor grudges. Instead, they don't hesitate to pick up the phone (or computer mouse) to make a call (or send an e-mail note) pointing out the problem immediately. Instead of waiting and allowing resentment to build up, solve the problem for yourself and the supplier as quickly as possible. After all, you want this to be a permanent relationship, so get rid of problems as they arise, or they will come back to haunt you.

5. View Your Supplier as an Ally

Guerrillas know that their suppliers might be ideal for a strategic alliance. Your supplier might go in with you on a mutual promotion, a special event, a publicity effort. Your supplier might even invest in your company, knowing the quality that you offer and how you cherish relationships.

Two key phrases

Keep two key phrases in mind in all of your supplier relationships: "long-term" and "mutual benefit." Both should serve as the foundation for all the business transacted between you and your suppliers. You are doing business with a particular supplier for the long run and not for the quick buck. You will continue to work together and profit together as long as there is mutual gain. If you make out like a bandit and your supplier just ekes out a small profit, you are missing the point. In all your dealings, take care to see that your supplier feels as rewarded and as happy about the relationship as you do. You don't want your suppliers to resent your success. Instead, you want them to share in it. And vice versa.

Your supplier relationships will fall neatly into place once you see each supplier as a long-term partner. Your business might become part of a tightly bonded network of other businesses, and one of your jobs will be to plug that supplier into the network. In return, you'll probably be connected to a few networks yourself. Everybody will gain—because everybody will attempt *to help*, not to squeeze, each other.

Benefits of close supplier relationships

When you have warm, close, trusting relationships with your suppliers, you will receive these benefits:

* Better prices
* Better service
* Availability of product when you need it
* Priority treatment
* Customized handling
* Immediate attention
* In-depth understanding of one another's problems and opportunities
* Kept promises
* Complete honesty
* Advance notice

These are only the surface ways in which you'll benefit. Perhaps the peace of mind of not having to constantly scour your community or industry for new suppliers will be the biggest benefit of all. And certainly you can't underestimate the power of trust between people.

Guerrilla entrepreneurs recognize that success comes not with sweeping and dramatic improvements but with tiny advantages in many areas, which tighten up and perfect all aspects of running a business. Having close relationships with suppliers is a way of capitalizing upon all possible benefits.

Firms that have a close relationship with suppliers have their fingers on the pulse of their industries. This keen insight provides them with the competitive edge that guerrillas hold so dearly. Every year in the United States, several million new businesses are launched. They have to seek out suppliers and then establish relationships with them—once they have learned that they can trust them. Only then can they begin to nurture that relationship to the point at which it can be considered close.

Fingers on the pulse

As a guerrilla entrepreneur, you'll have a battery of close supplier relationships. While your would-be competitors will be out beating the bushes in search of trustworthy suppliers, you'll probably be at the ballgame with yours. You'll be succeeding at business *and* having a good time—all at once. That's the way of the guerrilla entrepreneur.

13

Structuring Your Business

YOU'RE A GUERRILLA. You know the power of planning. You know the immense importance of priorities. You know your priorities, and you are determined to run your business by them. That's why it is crucial that you do certain things before you launch your business, before you start attracting customers, before you start on the guerrilla's path.

First, you must structure your business *before* you create it rather than *as* you create it, in a way that will enable you to achieve your goals.

When I urge you to do this, I do not refer to confirming the status of your business as a sole proprietorship, a partnership, or a corporation. The structuring that I am talking about has nothing to do with taxes or lawyers or board meetings. Instead it has to do with you and the determining of your priorities in life. As a guerrilla, it should be this: first comes life, and then comes business.

First comes life, and then comes business

When guerrillas structure their entrepreneurial enterprises, they make them accommodate the broad spectrum of life, not merely work. They structure them according to their priorities. Sure, their parents' priorities may have been a lot different, but times have changed. Living by priorities that are several generations old makes little sense as we zoom into a new millennium.

Here's an old riddle that used to be read to kids. If you could have a million dollars a day for a month or a penny the first day, two cents the next, and double the amount for each succeeding day of the month, which would you select?

If the month is February, the correct answer is a million

dollars a day because you'd end up with a snazzy $28 mil. But if
the month is January, the correct answer is a penny the first day
and double the amount each succeeding day. By the end of the
day on January 28, you'd have a bit less than $28 million. But at
the end of January, you'd have a whole lot more. On the thirti-
eth, you would have twice *that* amount. And on the thirty-first,
you'd have a large fortune.

*The last three
days of January* The reason I point this out is that figuratively, you are now
living during the last three days of January. The big payoffs
of research, education, technology, and science are *happening
right now.* As you are entering a new age, the new age is thrust-
ing itself upon you. So you'd better be ready to enter it. Structure your work to accommodate the new truths of an evolved
and enlightened society. These big breakthroughs are not only
technological. They are also social, governmental, and psychological. The guerrilla structures her business to take full advantage of these advancements, not to be bowled over by them.
She structures her entrepreneurial endeavor to capitalize upon
the new opportunities offered by the new age, and she knows
well that these opportunities represent merely the tip of the
evolutionary iceberg. But the guerrilla is prepared for more
change. Flexibility is her byword—for only the flexible can survive change.

*Structuring
your business,
guerrilla-style* The guerrilla entrepreneur structures a business before she
has earned one cent, so that as the business grows, it fits neatly
into the structure instead of outgrowing it. As the business gets
larger, the entrepreneur does not experience an increase in
stress, but rather a decrease, as wisdom replaces trial and error. If
you want to structure your business in a manner befitting the
twenty-first century, in a way that lets you cash in on the unreal
wealth of the "last three days," this is the framework to use:

1. Structure Your Business to Suit Yourself

Do you think that the earth revolves around the sun? In a large
sense, it certainly does, but in an even larger and more cogent
sense, it revolves around you. If you're delighted and everyone
around you feels the same, you're doing something right. And if

you're miserable, spreading misery in your wake, you are undoubtedly doing something wrong. One of the happiest people I know is an auto mechanic who was once a very unhappy lawyer.

The guerrilla entrepreneur structures a business around the intensely personal things that make that entrepreneur a unique individual. You must place yourself at the center of your business so that all of its components revolve around you. At the same time, you must place yourself above all the components, knowing that you as a person outrank anything about your business.

2. *Structure Your Business to Aim for Your Goals*

The purpose of your enterprise is to meet its goals. Clearly thought out goals at the outset put you on a track to success. You engage in nothing tangential to your goals, only in activities directed to helping you succeed. Because you have integrated your life with your business, the pursuit of your goals is a healthy endeavor, a price you willingly pay, a foreseen circumstance, a joy in your life. The perspective of your goals, clarified and illuminated by perfect focus, helps you stay on track with your business, helps you make many decisions, allows you to visualize what you must do even when your vision may be hazy or temporarily blocked.

That's the big reward when you have a goal. Even if you lose sight of it temporarily, it serves as true north on your entrepreneurial compass and magnetically guides you in the right direction.

3. *Structure Your Business to Accommodate Your Family*

This may be pretty simple if you have no family, but times change and you very well may have a family later. Over 90 percent of the CEOs of Fortune 500 firms are married. It seems *Go get married* to indicate that marriage and business success can be compatible. Even if you don't get married, you probably have important relationships with parents, siblings, living partners, or close friends.

Your business should be structured so that your family stays close to you, remembers your face, enjoys being with you, and does not resent your success. That success should be yours because of them and shared with them, not in spite of them.

Guerrillas structure their businesses so that their family never gets in the way of their work—and vice versa. They do not practice hard-core nepotism, though it is their prerogative. Instead, they are able to engage enthusiastically in their work without knocking over family members in their rush toward the goal line, without leaving cherished relationships in shattered pieces. Because they factored their family into their life and are able to see business as part of their life and not the entire reason for their existence, guerrillas maintain strong family ties, and they are able to love and be loved even though they are succeeding as entrepreneurs.

4. Structure Your Business to Suit Your Employees

Next to yourself and your family, the people who most want you to succeed in business—and who can do something about it—are your employees. Your business should be structured in a way that gives them room to grow, to flourish, to prosper as you prosper. Your business structure should provide a fertile ground for your employees to achieve their own goals as you achieve yours. It should balance humanity with capitalism, warmth with effectiveness, success with sensitivity. The guerrilla entrepreneur is a compassionate sort, honestly caring about employees—or independent contractors—almost as though they were members of the guerrilla's family. In a sense, they are, for they are motivated by similar goals, focused upon the same targets as the guerrilla.

All in the family

Guerrilla entrepreneurs treat two specific groups with respect, caring, and even reverence. Those groups are their customers and their employees. You already know my feelings about the glory of customers. I feel the same way about employees. No guerrilla enterprise should be structured in a way that does not reward employees for good work. Each enterprise should have optimum working conditions to promote high morale, employee loyalty, and inclusion in a future edition of *The 100 Best Places to Work in America*. Having worked at one of them, Leo Burnett Advertising in Chicago (and London), I experienced firsthand the bliss of working in an organization that was purposely structured to allow employees to create, produce, and flourish.

5. *Structure Your Business to Increase Your Profits*

In the century that is now passing, almost all businesses were structured to create profits ahead of everything else—the business owner, family, employees, and even company goals. Profits above all. But that was then. In this enlightened age, profits have a large role, but they are not the proof of success that they used to be. A guerrilla business is structured, without question, to maximize profits. But the profits grow without any sacrifice of the business owner's heart or soul, without exacting heavy payment from family or employees, without causing a proprietor to sell his soul and be diverted from his goals in pursuit of the hot, flashy buck. The guerrilla entrepreneur is extremely profit minded, knowing very well the difference between sales and profits.

The guerrilla also has a sense of pace and timing. This allows her to pursue short-term profits by some business actions and long-term profits by other avenues. By making the distinction between the short and the long run, the guerrilla is able to manage a small business while thinking like the owner of a large business. After all, most huge businesses started out as tiny entrepreneurial endeavors.

Pace and timing

6. *Structure Your Business to Take Advantage of the Technology of Today—and Tomorrow*

Guerrillas are quite friendly with current technology, not easily wooed by distant technological promises, and disdainful of obsolete technology. That's why in the initial structuring of a business, the guerrilla capitalizes on advancements in computers, marketing, communication, and his understanding of the behavioral sciences. Although the life span of technology grows shorter and shorter, and although some technologies thrive for a matter of six months before becoming outmoded, guerrillas realize that they are best off embracing what they can use right now even though it may become old-fashioned in a short time.

They know that by waiting for a computer's price to drop, they are losing money. While waiting for its speed to become faster or its memory larger, they are losing money. They recognize that they are better off riding a horse until the car is invented and then driving the car until the jet plane is invented. In all three cases, they get to their destination faster than if they had walked, and in all instances, they earn more money by using the present technology than by waiting for the prices to drop on the new. Can you imagine existing in today's society as a business without a computer? Millions of businesses are trying to do just that in an effort to save money. These businesses were not structured for existing technology. Their prospects for success are dim.

7. Structure Your Business with Geography in Mind

When I structured my first business, I did not factor in geography. So I ended up in a fancy corner office in a Chicago skyscraper, and I pulled in a fancy executive salary. But each winter, my ears nearly froze off on my way to and from that fancy office. And each winter I'd have to fly at least one thousand miles to do the skiing to which I am so addicted. Then, something happened to make me smart. I missed a bus and had to wait thirty minutes in a temperature of minus eighteen degrees.

"What am I doing here?" That's when I asked myself, "What am I doing here?" It didn't take long, because I had no adequate answer, for me to restructure my business for geography.

I still have the neat office, and my income is a lot higher than my salary was in Chicago, but winters are now joyous times for my ears. I don't even own earmuffs, and I have but a three-hour drive to the ski slopes of the Sierra. What's more, I look out of the window where I work to see one huge blue bay, two long bridges, three islands, countless mountains, and a sweeping panorama that keeps me fully aware that my geography is so dandy that heaven is a local call. The point is to ask yourself where you really want to live and then to become a guerrilla entrepreneur *there*, and not where you live now.

Guerrillas consider geography when assessing the competitive scene, the size of the job market in case they need employees, and the responsiveness of local government to small business. They factor in the weather, the commute, the overall atmosphere, and the opportunities for doing business globally, for working out of their own home, and for growth in the place where they intend to succeed.

8. Structure Your Business to Promote Growth and Diversification

At the beginning, you may want your business to be small and focused on a narrow area. Later, you may want to expand or add new products or services. But what if you're not structured for expansion or diversity? Tough luck, that's what.

Guerrilla businesses should foresee new economic conditions and the need for growth, so they plan their businesses to fill in niches when niches appear, to solve problems when problems arise. These businesses know they must walk before they run, so they are structured to begin small and then to grow or move into other areas. When the expansion takes place, everyone is ready rather than caught off guard. This happy state of affairs occurs because a guerrilla structured the business with future growth and diversification in mind. An anonymous business owner once said, "Change occurs only when my back's against the wall." Guerrillas, on the other hand, change when they feel like it, and when they are good and ready.

9. Structure Your Business to Maximize Your Passion

You feel glorious about the work you are doing right now. You look forward to work and enter a state of grace while you are doing it. Your passion fuels your fires, which burn intensely hot. That passion becomes translated into enthusiasm as it spreads throughout your company—to every one of your employees, and then, if you're playing your cards right, to your customers.

But perhaps you'll lose your passion. Somehow, the fire flickers and goes out. Then what? Do you continue doing the same thing? You'd better *not*, because if you lose your passion, your business will be in a lot of trouble. The fact is, you should seriously consider going into a different line of work. Without passion, you won't succeed at your goal of enjoying your work.

Guerrillas realize that they may lose their current spark and therefore structure their business so that there are other things for them to do, other activities about which they can become passionate. Those activities take place in the very same business. Is it a wild coincidence that they were available? Just the opposite. They are there because the business owner planned it that way. She structured her business so that when burnout took place, a new challenge would rise from the same business.

Never underestimate the power of passion, and never kid yourself as to whether or not you have it. If you burn out on manufacturing, move into sales. If you burn out on sales, move into service. If you burn out on service, move into administration. If you have no more passion for manufacturing, you'll be delighted that you structured your business to let you exercise your passion in another department. A close friend, serving as the president of his own company, found himself burned out completely by the chores of administration. So he turned the reins over to someone else and is now blissfully happy as a salesman. It's not easy to give up the presidency, but for him, it would have been folly to continue in that role.

10. Structure Your Business to Contribute to Your Planet

Three cheers for you, for your family, and for your employees! Now, let's hear a rousing cheer for planet earth! If the whole world is a bit too large for you, how about your own community? Guerrilla entrepreneurs know that they are citizens of the earth and of their community. They exist as individuals, as guerrillas, as members of their family, as part of the community, *and* as part of the whole world. They structure their businesses to let them enjoy all that guerrilla entrepreneurs would ever want to enjoy.

At the same time, noble causes such as improving the environ-　*Noble causes*
ment, helping the homeless, abetting the U.S. economy, teach-　*for guerrillas*
ing people to read, curing dread diseases, and bettering life for
children are beneficiaries of their business success as well. The
list of causes will continue forever, as will the need for the
business community to do something about them.

Perhaps your contribution to these noble causes will come
in the form of donating your product or service, making a cash
donation, or rolling up your sleeves and volunteering at a soup
kitchen. Whatever form your altruism takes, the important thing
is to nurture that sense of philanthropy and then activate it with
your business. It may sound difficult, but it's actually very easy if
you make it part of the overall structure of your business. Who-
ever heard of creating a small business with the idea of bettering
life on earth? Well, you have now, and guerrilla entrepreneurs
have been aware of the concept—even acted on it—for several
decades. In the coming millennium, giving back to your community or environment will prove to be less a choice for the
guerrilla entrepreneur, but a criterion for success.

The very notions of structuring a business with location in mind
or with your family factored in may seem far-fetched. But the
concept is foreign only to those whose thought processes are
mired in the past. Enlightened businesses of the present are
currently operating in ways that will benefit everyone—from the
owner of the business to a person in a distant land, who may
never hear of the business yet benefit from its success. Guerrilla
entrepreneurs preparing for the twenty-first century should follow this lead. It is the way of the guerrilla.

14

Structuring Your Time

IF YOU'RE ALREADY a guerrilla, you don't need to be reminded that time is not money. If time ever was money, it certainly isn't anymore. Time is far more important than money. If you run out of money, there are countless ways to scrounge up more. If you run out of time, it's R.I.P.

Just as crucial as structuring your business to succeed at its goals is the structuring of your time—your most important asset. You've got to devote enough of it to your work so that you can earn a living and enough of it to nonworking activities so that you can enjoy your life. Guerrillas integrate life and work, but work does not take up all their life.

The Roper poll, the Harris poll, the Gallup poll, and the Universities of Maryland and Pennsylvania conduct yearly studies to see what Americans cherish the most. It wasn't until 1988 that Americans finally came to their senses—and put time as the number one item on the list. Time has been number one every year since 1989 and will remain number one for the rest of our lives. It's astonishing that it took so long for us to place time in its proper perspective, but better late than never. At least guerrillas of the twenty-first century and beyond will know that time is decidedly *not* money and that it is a finite asset not to be squandered.

A nationwide study in 1996 conducted by *Adweek* magazine attempted to learn whether people would rather have free time or more money. Not surprisingly, 53 percent of the respondents said that they wanted free time. Among men, the choice of free time was made by 58 percent. Among people of ages twenty-five to thirty-four, 61 percent selected free time. Among those forty-five to fifty-five, time was chosen by 56 percent.

A recent Gallup poll revealed that the majority of Americans would rather work four days each week than five. Back in 1971, Americans actually preferred a five-day week. Slowly but surely, time is gaining stature.

Just as data will be the currency of the twenty-first century, time will be its most precious resource, *and everyone will know it*—you, your employees, your customers, your family. The more you can save time for these people, the more beloved a citizen of earth you will become. They will use the time you save them, according to one recent study, to be with their families, to travel, to study more, to compete at sports, and just to take it easy.

Everyone will know it

Ranked according to what people would do with their time, we learn that

* 15 percent would spend more time with their families.
* 11 percent would relax.
* 9 percent would travel.
* 6 percent would spend time with their hobbies.
* 6 percent would work around the house or garden.
* 6 percent would go back to school or study more.
* 5 percent would work more.
* 5 percent would hunt, fish, play golf or tennis, or camp out.
* 1 percent would read more.

Reverence for time is growing rapidly, and guerrilla-run companies must be prepared to honor it. Business strategies that save time for people help companies to grow *three times faster* and profit *five times more* than companies with strategies that ignore the crucial need for speed. Companies that were aware of time overran their markets, stole the best customers, increased the loyalty of the customers they already had, and became the leading industry innovators. Better still, their success all but closed off the business to competition. At best, only one or two competitors, moving as rapidly as they could, were able to stay in the game. The rest? Doomed.

The benefits of saving time for people

To structure your business as the guerrilla would, begin by making a list of the tasks that must be accomplished in order for you to score bull's-eyes on your targets. Some of these tasks may be handled by you if no one can do them better. Others must be delegated. Some are a pure joy for you to undertake. Others are pure pain. Structure your time so that you do the work that you do best and that excites you most. Allow others to do the rest. Someone will love to complete tasks that you find distasteful. No task must be ignored. No goal must be unattended to. Fitting yourself into the picture in the best possible way requires talent. You want your business to succeed, and yet you want to sacrifice none of your goals, one of which is enjoying life while you work and enjoying work while you live.

*Efficiency vs.
effectiveness* Before we investigate sane and intelligent ways for you to structure your time, let's clarify the distinction between efficiency, which is good, and effectiveness, which is very good. Efficient people are excellent at saving time, but shortsightedness often causes their efficiency to get in the way of their effectiveness. If someone was to pack a parachute for you and brag about how they were so efficient that it took them only ten seconds, you'd be leery about jumping from the airplane for fear that their effectiveness took a back seat to their efficiency.

But if someone else told you that they pack parachutes so effectively that not one has ever failed to open, you'd be a bit more confident wearing it during your plunge from the skies. You wouldn't give a hoot about efficiency and how rapidly the parachute was packed. So it should be for your guerrilla enterprise. Run it efficiently, to be sure, but never let efficiency get in the way of developing momentum that carries you toward your goals.

Effectiveness will carry you in the right direction. When structuring your time, remember that even though speed is a positive attribute, avoid it if it gets in the way of your overall effectiveness. Structure your time in order to accomplish the tasks that keep you on track, not whatever gets you down that track the fastest.

The guerrilla entrepreneur, although fascinated with ways of improving efficiency, is a real stickler about improving effectiveness and continually looks for methods of honing it. In *Zen and the Art of Motorcycle Maintenance*, the author, Robert Pirsig, was constantly working on his motorcycle, a labor of love, so that it never needed repairs. His mind was focused on the effectiveness of his machine and the pure enjoyment of working to improve it. If you consistently work on adding to the effectiveness of your earning endeavor, and if it is a labor of love, it will need few repairs.

Zen and the art of being a guerrilla

When structuring your time, keep in the forefront of your mind that the previously mentioned Gallup poll showed that nearly eight in ten adult Americans feel that time is moving too fast for them. Six of ten say they enjoy nonworking time the most, though 18 percent say they prefer being at work. More than five in ten bemoan the fact that they do not have the time to do the things that they really want to do. If you're to be the guerrilla I want you to be, you will be one of the two in ten Americans who feel that time is moving at a pace ideal for them; you will be one of the five in ten Americans who have the time to do everything they want to do. It won't happen by accident. And it won't happen because of luck.

It will happen because you structured your time to give yourself time. True, your business needs a lot of your time. But it does not need all of your time. The only entity that needs *all* of your time is you. Give generously of that time to your business, but don't be too lavish. Leave enough for yourself. When you structure your time properly, you will have the time that *you* need and the time that your *business* needs. You will never sacrifice company profitability to get extra time. That extra time will be built into your existence.

Where do you begin when structuring your time? A good but not very obvious place is *yourself* and your own style. Although research into sleep and wakefulness continues at an increasing pace, we still have much to learn. But we do know that some people operate best starting early in the morning and then slow down in the early evening, whereas others are just getting started in the early evening. Darkness is when they are at their brightest.

It is difficult to lead a life of going against your natural grain, forcing your body clock to say tock-tick, tock-tick—so if you hate getting up in the morning, you ought to sleep late and capitalize on your natural energy in the late afternoon. If your business requires a morning presence, and you love sleeping until noon, you may have to delegate your duties to someone else during that time. If it requires someone to be around at night, and you're in dreamland at dusk, let somebody else run your show— or be clear on the times you will be on hand.

My clients and associates know never to call me early in the morning because I'll be sleeping or reading the paper. They know never to call me on Thursdays or Fridays because I'll be away hiking, skiing, or exploring by automobile. They know I never answer the phone during the evenings. And they're aware that the worst times of all for calling me are Monday, Tuesday, and Wednesday afternoons, when I'm hardest at work. So they contact me at the times that fall in between the cracks, they keep conversations brief, and they make intelligent use of my answering machine and e-mail, eliminating the necessity for much face-to-face contact. I've got nothing against face-to-face contact, but I've got a strong leaning toward inner fulfillment.

Guerrillas structure their time according to their *priorities.* They do not think in terms of nine to five, but instead in terms of accomplishing goals. And they are dramatically different from their counterparts in their ability to *delegate,* to cover their act.

Delegating is a word that everybody knows, but few people practice delegation with skill. Guerrillas are masters at passing the buck. To be as adept as they are, to put your delegating money where your delegating mouth is, consider the following ideas:

1. Recognize that every time you delegate successfully, you are doubling your own effectiveness.
2. Unless a task is your passion, don't do it if you can delegate it. Recognize that you are delegating not only work but also responsibility for results.

3. Don't delegate a task to someone who won't do the work as well or better than you can do it.

4. Don't delegate a task to someone if you're not willing first to train that person to do the job with excellence.

5. Don't always tell the person to whom you are delegating *how* to achieve the results. Just talk about the results to encourage initiative.

6. Don't limit the concept of delegating only to work chores; consider it also for the multitude of home chores. Time is time, always precious.

7. When delegating, provide as much information about the task as possible, but don't overload a person with data.

8. When you delegate, be sure that you also delegate the authority to make the necessary related decisions. Let the person to whom you delegate set the terms, timetables, and objectives so he or she can measure how the work is going.

9. Tell the truth about a task to the person to whom you delegate it. If it is drudgery, don't say that the task is glamorous.

10. If you don't know how to trust, you'll have problems delegating. True guerrillas have the ability to trust others with territory and power.

* * *

When you elevate your delegating skills to the level that work delegated is work accomplished *better* than you would have done it, you'll be able to structure your business to be compatible with your nature. This invaluable talent will set you apart from entrepreneurs of the past.

Mastering the art of delegation puts you in control of your time, instead of the reverse. Instead of being dictated by your boss, your clients, your community, and tradition, your time can be governed by different priorities—your own.

Structure Your Time Around Yourself

Guerrillas know when and how they function best, and then arrange their schedule so that they can make their optimum contributions when they are at their peak. They know the importance of energy, vitality, and enthusiasm, and they know they will shortchange their work if they produce the most when they have the least to give. Their entire business plan is designed for *enlightened selfishness*. Peak performance is the result.

Structure Your Time Around Your Goals

Now that you've accommodated your strengths and style in structuring your business, you can devote attention to your skills as an entrepreneur. Match the operations of your business to your goals as closely as you can. You have honestly clarified your goals. You have been realistic. Structure your time to help you achieve those goals in the most effective manner possible. The way that things used to be done may not be the way they should be done now. Focus on attaining all your objectives.

Structure Your Time Around Your Family or Friends

Your kids' growing up is a one-time performance. There are no encores. The good old days are happening now, and they include a lot more than your financial survival. Youth isn't wasted on the young when the young have their priorities on straight and refuse to allow their earning-a-living time to interfere with their living time. Business schools don't encourage entrepreneurs to structure their time to include family and friends, but they will in time. Why should you learn this lesson the hard way?

Structure Your Time Around Your Profits

Almost certainly, pursuit of the good old dollar bill will be one of your goals, so when you structure your limited time in this universe, be sure to direct a goodly portion of it toward amassing profits. Those profits may not come instantly, but when you do begin to generate them, they should increase in size every month if you're going about things right. That means you're getting wiser every month and learning from mistakes every month, and that your time is well planned. The reality of dealing with people in different time zones, nationally and globally, makes an impact on how you will structure your time. Yet it is possible to have time for yourself, your goals, your friends and family, and still turn a steadily increasing profit. One way is with delegating. The other is with technology.

Structure Your Time with Technology

In the not very distant past, the best time-saver we had was a good grasp of time management—planning, making lists, prioritizing. That is still an ally of the guerrilla entrepreneur, but powerful new forces have joined the battle for time—and the most potent is technology. Technology has presented to time-conscious entrepreneurs a glorious selection of time-savers: computers, e-mail, fax machines, answering devices, pagers, car phones, air phones, hands-free phones, and even microwaves and books on tape. By incorporating this technology into your business modus operandi, along with the art of delegating, you will be able to structure your time in this evolved way.

Technology to the rescue

Are there really people who can be successful entrepreneurs while avoiding the traps of workaholism and early burnout? Yes, they already exist. Do these people actually succeed while structuring their time according to the guidelines in this chapter? Yes, and success comes to them even more easily because of how they have eliminated unnecessary stress from their lives.

More of those people succeed now than ever before in history. There will be more of them in the next ten years than there are now. These suggestions for structuring your time sound impractical for today's world, but much of today's world is yesterday's world. These suggestions are for tomorrow's world, guideposts that mark the guerrilla's way.

Entrepreneurs playing by the rules of the past run the risk of dying with regrets for things they have not tried. While I lived in England, I had a friend who was a Catholic priest, eighty-one years old. One day he said that the thing that surprised him most about his calling was something he had learned while taking the final confession of people about to die. He said that none of them ever expressed regrets for things they had done. They only regretted things that they *hadn't* done.

My friend said he didn't want to die with any of those regrets. And he lived his life so that he didn't. Now that you are aware of the land of the possible, I hope you don't leave this world regretting that you didn't try your skill by walking the guerrilla's trail.

15

Working from the Virtual Office Called Home

BE IT EVER so humble, there's no place like virtual home. Of the many simultaneous revolutions going on or recently completed—the computer revolution, information revolution, digital revolution, and communications revolution—one of the most important is the virtual revolution. It's as fundamental and sweeping as the best of them. And it offers you a quantum leap in productivity.

A 1996 People's Network TV report revealed that by the year 2000, one-third of the homes in America will be housing a home-based business. But the revolution of working at home is no day at the beach. For all the joys, there's at least one misery— the lack of social togetherness with coworkers. Yet the survival rate of home-based businesses is surprisingly high. One study from 1992 revealed that 74.6 percent of people who had started a home-based business three years earlier were still in business—and 71.2 percent were in the exact business they had started, now grown larger.

It is easier than ever to succeed while working from home, which guerrilla entrepreneurs tend to do, because they enjoy avoiding a commute and because of breakthroughs in communication (e-mail, fax machines, voice mail, teleconferencing, and pagers). An executive with Sea-Land Corporation, a $3.5 billion shipping company in New Jersey, says, "All I need is a personal computer to track any of the 1.2 million shipping containers we have in our computer system. I can do that just as well from my house as I can from a high-rise office overlooking the docks. Who needs to be near the ships?" A good question for all guerrillas.

Three waves of change have drawn workers from their city offices to suburban or even mountaintop home workplaces. The first change came in the 1950s, when manufacturers took their huge factories out of settled areas and put them wherever electric power lines and railroads could reach. The second change was the final burst of construction of the interstate highway system in the 1970s, which served as a convenient conduit to escape the city. And the third wave of change was the fiber-optic wave of the 1990s, which in ten years will complete a network greater in scope than the interstate system, which took half a century to build. It connects all phones, modems, and computers into a communication/information/social superhighway. And still another wave, the wireless wave, is approaching.

For dramatic evidence that it is no longer necessary to "be near the ships," consider that one of the largest and fastest-growing computer companies, Dell Computer, has no location anywhere—no headquarters, no offices. It is a virtual computer company, consisting of toll-free phone lines and a chain of United Parcel Service trucks linked by radio-equipped computers.

America is growing so virtual and so many people are working from home that the number of telecommuters has *quadrupled* since 1990. This migration to the home is the result of a downsizing frenzy that forced more than 4 million white-collar workers out of their jobs. Adding to the momentum of the migration is technology, which makes working from home much simpler. Still another reason for the emergence of home-based businesses is the decentralizing of huge companies. Business authority Peter Drucker says that the role of middle management in a corporation has been that of a data conduit, passing information down from executives and up from workers. But this information, now in the domain of a mainframe computer, is dispersed to a network of inexpensive desktop machines. Goodbye, middle management.

Working from home is not always pure joy when you con- *Not always*
sider that *pure joy*

* The United States is still woefully unprepared for the demands that will be made by a virtual economy. Many lending institutions still can't find it in their hearts to make loans
  to businesses without storefronts or reception areas.
* Our communications infrastructure is unprepared to deal
  with the sort of broadband information gathering and dis-
  semination needed. Everyone and their neighbor needs
  phone lines for their phones, fax machines, and modems,
  and the phone lines aren't in place yet. Like the interstate
  highway, they'll take time to get connected.
* Our legal system works against business relationships and is
  too slow to deal with the contractual needs of fast-growing
  companies. Speed has never been a hallmark of the legal
  world.
* Our government has only the barest notion of the Internet
  and the implications of virtual businesses. The Internet is
  growing fast, but it's still tiny compared to the enormous size
  it's going to attain.
* Developing a virtual corporation will be one of the biggest
  challenges you will ever face because it goes against what
  you were taught in school and even by past experience. But
  the literature and the technology are improving. And being
  a pioneer isn't supposed to be a cinch.

Still, the list of companies that have successfully gone virtual is long and impressive:

* Atlas Industrial Door
* Benetton
* Cincinnati Milacron
* Corning Glass
* Cypress Semiconductor
* DuPont
* Eastman Kodak

* General Electric
* General Mills
* Hewlett-Packard
* Lenscrafters
* Levi Strauss
* Motorola
* NCR
* Otis Elevator
* Wal-Mart

I have been working from home since 1971. I can think of no other existence that can match it. Except for the computer and printer, you'd have a hard time telling my office from my dining room. After training my daughter to understand that her daddy worked from home and that if she made noise after school and her daddy couldn't work, we would be banished to the poorhouse—or worse, Chicago in the winter—I found that working from home had zero disadvantages.

For the investment in office equipment, I never needed a lump sum. Instead, I made the investment over the years. Fortunately, in the work I've done, I never needed truly expensive stuff. One by one I picked up a typewriter (now in my antique cabinet), computer, printer, fax machine, scanner, answering machine, modem, file cabinet, desk, and cordless phone. Not a lot of stuff. Luckily, I've been in the kinds of business that work perfectly from a home: consultant, ad maker, author, columnist, and speaker.

The discipline To work at home means I've got to have the discipline to
to ignore things ignore all the things that I love so much: the pool, the puppy, the cats, the refrigerator, my wife, and the enticements of nature. Not paying attention to such diverting enticements isn't easy, but I save so much on the rent and commuting that it's worth the effort. Guerrillas are ever-alert for ways of *creating* time. If they can develop a business that saves them the time most people spend commuting, it is like adding 433 days to their lives (based upon a one-hour, one-way commute and a twenty-year lag time

between starting the commute and realizing that you should never commute another day in your life). Time is not money, and it is not a commuting opportunity either.

Paul and Sarah Edwards, who have authored a series of excellent books about working at home, alert us to the seven worst at-home mistakes:

The worst at-home office mistakes

1. Jumping In Too Soon

Working at home is not a theory, but a practice, and until you practice it, you won't know the miseries or joys. So you should investigate it by talking with others, being with them in their home office, temping for them, or doing something to show you their day-to-day routine. The more similar the business is to yours, the greater your insight into the rewards and hassles.

2. Unprofessional Marketing

People try to juggle their entrepreneurial enterprise with their selling efforts and with their marketing, which they try to do themselves, and the result can be a disaster. Marketing is a game that involves money, even though many marketing weapons are free. Play this game to win, and that means going about it with a strategy and with professionalism.

3. Underpricing Your Work

This occurs when you underestimate your costs. Be sure to include in your charges every single cent that was spent for you to do the work, and that includes the cost of the home office. When you calculate the cost of your work, it should provide enough to cover costs, help you meet household and personal expenses, and return a tidy profit. It should also be competitive, which may be even a bit more expensive than others because of your unique niche.

4. The Wrong Name

The Edwardses tell us that many people who start home businesses pick unprofessional names. They use their kids' names or pick one that starts with an *A* so they can be up front in the Yellow Pages. Consider these naming tips:

* Pick one that's easy to pronounce, spell, and remember.
* Pick one that describes your business and, if possible, a competitive advantage.
* Pick one that doesn't remind people of any other existing businesses.
* Pick one that is catchy, but not overclever; people want results, not laughs.
* Pick one that does not prohibit you from expanding or diversifying.

5. No Listing in the Phone Directory

Listen, people lose phone numbers, misplace business cards, and forget things. If people are used to finding businesses like yours in the Yellow Pages, you must be there. If not, you should at least be in the white pages. And remember that your Yellow Pages ad is supposed to bring in phone calls, not compliments on the ad. Chapter 15 of *Guerrilla Marketing for the 90s* is devoted entirely to giving guerrillas advice about the Yellow Pages.

6. Making a Tax Blunder

It's never fun to have the IRS frown at your return, but as one who works from home, you will draw added attention and usually be required to pay estimated taxes on a quarterly basis. If you don't do this, later on you are charged big penalties that come right out of your profits. Home office deductions can be generous and can be tricky. It's worth the expense to get a tax pro to help you tiptoe through this home business minefield.

7. Faulty Equipment Decisions

As a rule of thumb, spend money on office equipment that will help you increase your revenue. Recognize that using a computer is equivalent to having two to three extra employees or independent contractors. Although the technology changes as quickly as every five months, get the newest model you can; stick with well-known brands, and be sure your computer—all office equipment for that matter—can be easily serviced.

Wired magazine asked a panel of five experts in 1995 when they thought 20 percent of the workers in the United States will be workers from home. Two authorities said it would be 1999. Another said 2000. A fourth said 2005, and the fifth said 2010. The average prediction for this telecommuting landmark was the year 2003. Yet the 1996 TV report mentioned in the opening of this chapter said that 33 percent of U.S. workers would be at home on the job by 2000. The pace is staggering. And the *Wired* experts said the number of home workers would triple during the next fifteen years.

In that same issue, *Wired* asked the same experts when the Fortune 500 would welcome a virtual corporation into its ranks. The answers ranged from 1997 to never, with the average prediction being 1999. Right now, in 1996, 9.6 million Americans consider themselves to be telecommuters—perceiving themselves plugged into that category by virtue of the networked computers and cellular telephones that enable them to work outside their office. Experts say that telecommuting, even when family circumstances don't make it necessary, saves you about $1,000 a year when you consider wear and tear on your car, clothing appropriate for work, and lunches.

A Fortune 500 virtual corporation

The issue of loneliness while working at home is one that you should seriously address. Some experts believe that working at home can lead to a feeling of employee isolation and a reality of bureaucratic ineffectiveness.

The spectacular growth curve of working from home is paralleled by the growth of the neighborhood coffee shop industry. Think Starbucks to get an idea of what I'm talking about. One of the main reasons that coffee shops are growing at such a rapid pace is because people get lonely working all by themselves. They need a place where they can engage in the social

Loneliness and coffee shops

interaction they used to know at work. Along with cream and sugar, the coffee shop provides social life and networking opportunities to go with your coffee.

Be sure you build time into your week to interact with others, connect with your independent allies, gab on the phone, do things to beat the lonelies. There is no rule that says when working at home you must be lonely, must work long hours, must work deep into the night, must sacrifice your effectiveness, or must work alone. Guerrilla entrepreneurs make up their own rules so that they reap the benefits but do not suffer the consequences of working from home.

16

Being as Flexible as
You Have to Be

ORIGINALLY, THIS CHAPTER was entitled "Being as Flexible as You Can Be," but I decided that that title would lead you astray. Simply being as flexible as you can be, as a business owner, is not going to be enough for consumers in the next century. They're going to expect you to be as flexible as *they* want you to be. So you've got to be prepared to do a lot of bending and twisting. Quality is now taken for granted, and consumers will differentiate between companies based on their flexibility.

To you, flexibility will mean the ability to *operate in ranges*. You must offer prospective customers a range of products, a range of services, a range of prices, a range of places where they can visit you. You must plan to be flexible at the very start, so that future requests for you to bend don't break you.

The key to being flexible is connecting with sources that provide complementary products, services, prices, and amenities. These sources may be allied businesses, independent contractors, or employees—anyone who can extend your range. If you are flexible to the maximum, meaning that you are able to say yes to every request, your prospects and customers will never be disappointed. Last night, my wife needed a prescription from the pharmacy long after the delivery hours were over. She called their service, and forty-five minutes later, the prescription was delivered. That's flexibility, and that's why Marin Center Pharmacy has been our pharmacy for over twenty years.

Recently, a woman from North Carolina read an article

about me in *Inc.* magazine. She then invited me to speak at a conference she was hosting later that month, but it was short notice because the original speaker had canceled out. Bummer. I was going to be away on a desert vacation. But bummer *not*—I was able to direct her to the president of Guerrilla Marketing International, who could arrange for another speaker on the topic to appear at her conference. The day was saved for her, for me, for the other speaker, because of flexibility. It wasn't so much that I personally was flexible, but that my company was.

As you read this, flexibility is the major competitive advantage for many companies in Japan. In that country, quality has come to be the price of admission, so the Japanese have *got to have flexibility* simply to stay in the game. This is fast becoming the reality for American businesses too.

Quality was the international byword in the 1980s. In the 1990s, it is *flexibility*. In the first ten years of the twenty-first century, it will be *innovation*. Operating in the here and now, guerrillas concentrate upon being the most flexible providers in the land. They already have quality down pat. Of course, they also have several innovative plans for the future. But right now, they are focusing upon flexibility, and they apply it in many areas:

Where guerrillas are flexible

Production Processes

Because innovation will be a hallmark of the future, your production processes will be forced to change in order for you to keep your competitive advantages. Most production process improvements come in the areas of adding speed or economy, so your offerings will have to pass these benefits on to your customers. The only way to do it is to structure your production processes to be flexible. If you don't yet offer an economy-size version of your offering, you'll make changes so that you do.

Shipping Procedures

Because customers are increasingly aware that time is more precious than money, they'll be in a hurry to receive what they just bought from you, be it product or service. Where two-day service was once acceptable, and then upgraded to overnight service by customer demand, same-day service is now the preferred rate of receipt. Thanks to computers and the Internet, same-day service can become "right now" service. Things that used to be shipped in boxes—books, tapes, CDs, magazines—can now be shipped in bits electronically by computer through phone lines. Delivery has never been more instant. Guerrillas have to be flexible enough to accommodate the public's expectations of speed.

Supplier Relations

Very often, a guerrilla can only be as fast as her supplier. The sign of a true guerrilla is very fast delivery due to very fast-acting suppliers. Guerrillas don't maintain business relationships with slow-moving suppliers. Instead, they arrange ahead of time for the priority treatment of their account, hence their customers. Guerrillas develop such close relationships with their suppliers that no deliveries are late, no supplier is tardy. Guerrillas deal only with like-minded suppliers who understand the need for speed. What's more, guerrillas may even have entered into a strategic alliance with a supplier. This pays off in closer guerrilla-supplier and guerrilla-customer relations and, for the guerrilla, more flexibility.

Customer Relations

The rubber meets the road in the area of customer relations. It's where lack of flexibility gets punished the most severely in the form of customers taking their business elsewhere, and where it gets rewarded the most lavishly in the form of customers placing more orders and suggesting that their friends do the same. When the computer technician comes to work on my computer at night, when I'm not using it, I consider him a paragon of flexibility and recommend his service to others. It may be no big deal to him, for he thinks like a guerrilla, but to me it means no downtime and no dismantling of the computer to bring it to him.

Hours of Operation

Businesses must be open when their customers most need them . to be. At first, this may seem like a task requiring monumental flexibility, but once it is part of the overall business plan, and once you have connected with people—employees, independent contractors, or other business owners who can fill in while you are out—your hours of operation will better match the needs of your customers. Those guerrillas for whom the Internet is relevant can offer customers twenty-four-hour access to their services. The Internet is changing the entire concept of when businesses are open and when they're closed.

Happily, companies in the twenty-first century will not have to offer much flexibility in prices, though it will help a business to have both high-end and low-end offerings. The era of set prices is already dawning in the automotive industry. The public seems to love it, even though prices are not flexible. Most people dislike price haggling. Instead of price reductions, customers will seek added values in the form of better service, higher quality, more innovative features—and especially, more flexibility. Flexibility, just like superb service, means whatever the customer wants it to mean. And you, as a guerrilla, want the customer to have whatever he or she wants. When your company takes into account the demand for flexibility, offering it should not be a strain.

Enemies of
flexibility
    The enemies of flexibility are bureaucracies, company policies, being in a rush, moving too slowly, insensitivity, and employees who do not revere the opportunity to be flexible. The allies of flexibility are speed, good organization, not being in a rush, sensitivity, and a desire for profits.

In which areas should you become more flexible? *Ask your customers.* Send out questionnaires to determine in which areas your customers would appreciate more flexibility. *Shop your competitors.* See if they are offering any flexibility you aren't offering. *Study your industry.* Someone must be setting new standards in flexibility if it's not you. Learn who it is, and then offer the same or even more flexibility than they do.

Think about the businesses you patronize most often. When you consider flexibility, which of those businesses spring to mind? None of them? One of them? Probably none or very few have established a niche for flexibility because it is still such a new offering in the business world. In an era when companies need all they can to set them apart, guerrilla entrepreneurs sweeten all their offerings with flexibility. A guerrilla's connections with cooperating businesses are plentiful, and his favorite thing to say to a customer or prospect is "yes."

In adapting to the twenty-first-century mode of business, guerrillas should examine all the components of their business, customer related or not, and then determine in which areas flexibility can be an asset. A functional business plan allows a business to allocate resources—money, people, time—to multiple uses. This opens the door to more opportunities, and because guerrillas are by nature fast on their feet and able to take action, they will capitalize upon these.

How many businesses have started to fall behind by not embracing the Internet? How many have faltered because they didn't want to take all credit cards? How many have lost out because they didn't have a toll-free number? The most important question is this: *why* didn't these businesses take advantage of these advancements in the American Way of Doing Business? The most obvious answer is that they *lacked flexibility.* Even though it was easy to make the decisions to move forward with these profit builders, it was hard to incorporate them into the way business was being done at the time.

Guerrillas investigate five aspects of their customer service to make them more flexible:

1. Speed
2. Reliability

3. Punctuality
4. Communication
5. Delivery

Market your flexibility

The guerrilla entrepreneur must find ways not only to offer more flexibility, but also to market that flexibility. To do this, focus specific advertisements or direct mail upon your business's unique flexibility. Use it as a shining competitive advantage. An auto detailing company once sent me a postcard that said "Your place or ours?" and then explained that they work at their garage or the customer's home. That's what I call flexible. Guerrillas also scrutinize their own products to improve them with flexibility, looking into

1. Size
2. Shape
3. Availability
4. Engineering
5. Cost

Nurturing cooperation, obliterating competition

Realizing that business is a blend of nurturing cooperation while obliterating competition, guerrillas outflank their competitors with ideas, imagination, and creativity, applying their brainpower to the five areas I've just listed, plus countless more that I haven't. Remember, although guerrillas map their success with a definite plan, that plan has been made with an erasable pencil, and there's an eraser in their pocket. As a guerrilla in the twenty-first century, that eraser will keep your business flexible.

PART III

The Tools

E VEN GUERRILLA ENTREPRENEURS can't achieve their goals using their bare hands. They need help. They need tools. Some of these tools are in their own minds—such as the ability to focus. Others are living, breathing implements for success in the form of people—employees, independent contractors, or strategic alliance partners. And still others are the guerrillas themselves—or, rather, *first-class versions* of them.

One of the most crucial tools is one that you can't see or touch, but is becoming increasingly valuable with time. It's data, and it's getting easier to get *and* easier to filter.

Certainly the tools for making it with your own business in the twenty-first century include the tools of technology. The technologies available are becoming more ubiquitous, easier to use, lower in cost, and nearly mandatory. Technologies connect guerrillas with other people, ideas, and things, enabling them to avail themselves of the tool of global unity. Opportunities that were not even imaginable during most of the twentieth century exist all over the world now—because of the collapse of trade barriers and the creation of the Internet.

Because the entrepreneurial spirit runs rampant on the planet, guerrillas utilize the tool of strategic alliances, temporarily partnering with others who can help advance them toward mutually agreed goals. The more of these tools that the guerrilla uses—half of them are free—the better prepared she is to survive, prosper, and achieve her own goals while surmounting tough challenges. All the while, the guerrilla makes it look easy because she has all the right tools.

As with all other aspects of succeeding as a guerrilla entrepreneur, the tools of the twenty-first century will be a harmonious blending of the tools of the past (focusing and people) with the tools of the future (technology and global relationships). The way of the guerrilla will always be characterized by acute vision, both backward and forward, a 360-degree perspective that will provide the ideal tools for the times.

17

The Need to Focus

THE FIRST GUERRILLA TOOL available to you is your own mind and its ability to focus on your goals and on the tasks at hand—an ability that will serve your business now and in the twenty-first century. To a guerrilla, focusing starts at the beginning of going into business and never stops, as the entrepreneur sees the bull's-eye with increasing clarity. Your focus is provided in your business plan, simple to understand and to follow.

Most people want to follow a business plan, but they can't because their focus is diverted because of the constant inevitable need to solve petty problems. They are putting out fires instead of planting seeds. Sometimes they even lose their focus completely, too carried away by distractions and failure to remember the purpose of their business in the first place. The guerrilla solution to these distractions is reading your mission statement repetitively. This does not mean you should read it daily, but it does mean you should read it regularly. It sounds simplistic, but as a guerrilla in the ever-competitive market of the twenty-first century, you must remind yourself of the reason you went into business in the first place and the direction in which you want to proceed.

As repetition is the key to effective marketing and no-nonsense sales training, it also unlocks the barrier to focus. Yes, yes, I know that you have read your business plan and know your mission. But if you have failed to focus or been diverted for even an instant, you don't really know your mission. Perhaps your conscious mind knows the lyrics, but your unconscious doesn't know the melody.

Unlocking the barrier to focus

Unfortunately, in most businesses, day-to-day activities take priority status over everything else. Because reviewing the company focus is not usually a day-to-day event, business owners slowly lose sight of it, take it for granted, digress from their prime purpose. And don't think that printing out the plan and framing it will do much good. Instead, it'll soon become part of the decor rather than the constant tangible reminder it needs to be.

Instead, everyone connected with the company, including suppliers and strategic partners, must be made aware of the plan and the need to stay the course. If everyone knows the right direction, it is more difficult to get lost. Maintaining focus is often a matter of teamwork. To do this, some guerrillas begin each meeting with a reading of their mission statement.

More than a ritual

Rereading your plan will implant your mission statement in your unconscious mind, where your best ideas and most powerful motivation come from. If you're not enlisting that megaforce in your quest to achieve entrepreneurial nirvana, you're fighting an uphill battle. Writing your business plan is more than a ritual. It is also the creation of a road map, and if you're lost for an instant, that road map can prevent you from getting more lost. Your unconscious mind is one of the most valuable tools in your guerrilla arsenal. Tap as much of it as you can with the proven power of repetition.

Many businesses have no clue as to what they should focus on. Guerrilla entrepreneurs know there are *three specific areas* upon which their gaze must be narrowly focused:

* *Their own reason for being.* Knowing that writing things down hones their focus, guerrillas prepare a written statement of their purpose. It is in on paper and in their hearts at all times.
* *Their potential target markets.* They want to achieve maximum profitability and so they carefully select the markets that will help fulfill that goal, realizing they may have multiple targets.
* *Their market niche.* This means focusing on their customers,

their prospects, their competitors, and the realities of their marketplace.

What, exactly, does focus do for an entrepreneur? It keeps the goals in sight, and those goals are the bright light that illuminates the way for the company. Focus changes "what might be" into "what will be." Many entrepreneurial, freedom-loving types are wandering spirits, free souls carried by chance and opportunity to wherever the winds blow. Guerrillas know that goals leave nothing to chance. Goals force you to be specific. And focus keeps the goals in clear view. *What focus does*

You hear daily horror stories of failed businesses, and you wonder how you can succeed while others have fallen by the wayside. The way to do it is to set goals and focus on them. Here's a depressing statistic: *only 2 percent* of the population puts their goals into writing. This number certainly doesn't depress guerrillas. Instead, they are encouraged by it because it indicates the low level of competition out there. Of course businesses are going to fall on their capitalistic faces if they have no written goals.

Never state as a goal something you do not believe in. In order to keep that goal in clear focus, you must believe in your heart that it will happen. You must be able to visualize it. More than one wise guerrilla has said, "If you can visualize it, you can will it, and if you can will it, you can achieve it."

If failure to focus is the number one reason for business failure, and if not having goals leads to focus failure, why don't more people set goals in the first place? Terri Lonier, in her terrific book *Working Solo*, gives three reasons: *Why people don't set goals*

1. Fear of Embarrassment at Not Reaching Their Goals

Lonier quotes motivational speaker Tony Robbins as saying, "Success comes from good judgment, which comes from experience. But where does experience come from? Bad judgment. The only failure is if you stop. If you quit, you're sure not to succeed."

Everyone who has achieved greatness has experienced failure. Thomas Edison failed over forty times. If he was embarrassed at those failures, we might still be groping in the dark. Hockey great Wayne Gretzky said, "You miss 100 percent of the shots you never take." As one who has been an entrepreneur of the guerrilla variety for a quarter of a century, I'd say that failure and embarrassment, stumbling and falling are part of the entrepreneurial deal and some of the reasons that eventual success tastes so sweet.

2. Fear of Never Being Able to Change Your Goals Once You've Set Them

Although commitment to your goals increases the likelihood of bringing them to happy fruition, those goals belong to you, and you don't belong to them. Just as you have set them, you may change them. Often, changing is a foolish thing to do, and brilliant plans are abandoned because of an unnecessary change in goals. But there are occasions when change is prudent. Remember that this section of the book is about *tools*, not about *laws*, and that flexibility is a necessity in an entrepreneurial career. Your goals are your slaves, not your masters. With time and new insight, you probably will alter your goals because you've become smarter. Only with focus will you know if and when to make changes.

3. Fear of Not Having the Ability or Not Being Worthy Enough to Reach Your Goals

One of the main reasons people don't set goals is because of low self-esteem. They underestimate their own power and probably have no inkling of the power of their unconscious minds. Others figure that if they do accomplish their goals, they will be expected to work at that level all the time, something that is not part of their dream. Still more fear the rejection of outsiders who they imagine might be doubting them, thinking, "Who do you think you are?"

*   *   *

Now that she has scared us witless at the reasons people do not set goals, the good Ms. Lonier comes to our rescue, and clues us in on the magic ingredients for selecting goals that can be focused upon with ease, as well as attained.

How to set goals

1. Set Specific Goals

Don't say "Our business will grow" when you can say "Our business will grow at 20 percent per year for the first five years." Use numbers. Give dates. Set goals that may be broken down into little chunks so that you can move systematically. Remember that a marathon is only a series of connected steps, made one at a time. Connect visual images with your goals because if you can see them, they will be much easier to achieve.

2. Put Your Goals into Words

You can focus easily on words that you can read. Although you may know in your heart what your goals are, give your heart the benefit of your brain and your visual sense. Some successful guerrillas think that putting goals on paper is the most important step to attaining them. A famous study of the Yale University class of 1953 revealed that only 3 percent of the class had committed their goals to paper. Twenty years later, subsequent research among the same students showed that the 3 percent had achieved more financial success than the remaining 97 percent of their classmates combined.

3. Review Your Goals Regularly

This alone will help you keep your goals in constant focus. Guerrillas actually set aside time regularly to review, assess, and evaluate their goals. This keeps them on track, measures their performance, and prevents them from being intimidated by lofty goals. Experts call this "managing your goals"—changing them as you change and as your business changes, ideally keeping their thrust alive.

*   *   *

Daily, planes leave the San Francisco Bay area, where I live, bound for Hawaii. That is their goal. As they begin their journey across the Pacific, how many stay precisely on course? *None.* But focusing on their goal helps them make minute adjustments that get them exactly where they planned to go. And if guerrillas are piloting the aircraft, they're enjoying the journey.

18

People — the Life Force of Any Business

THE LATE Leo Burnett, my mentor and idol and the founder of what I believe was the finest advertising agency on earth (maybe ever), used to say: "Each day, our inventory goes up the elevator. Each night it goes down." Before that, I hadn't thought of myself as inventory.

Still, inventory is what I was, and no matter what kind of business you're in, your inventory also consists of human beings — yourself, your independent-contractor partners, and your employees. Those humans are the life force that makes your business thrive. The difference between a good worker and a bad worker can make the difference between your business failing or succeeding.

Each person connected with your business increases or decreases your profitability. That's pretty simple. A mediocre employee may have no visible effect on your profits, but no effect actually translates into a loss because you are in business to make a profit, not to tread water. The guerrilla establishes connections with people who can help business prosper. These people can actually increase *your* profitability because of *their* efforts.

The only way you're going to benefit from these people is to let them know, before you connect with them, that you are expecting them to help increase your profitability. Running a profitable operation is part of *your* agenda. This may not be part of *their* agenda at all, so you've got to get them, by helping them understand your mission, to put your collective profits on their agenda. Sure, you might be able to help them take this perspective later, but guerrillas go for birds in the hand over birds in the bush anytime.

Strangely enough, and I guess it's not so strange after all, everything boils down to humanity. When you are about to connect with a person, as a member of your network or an employee, the time-honored advice is to hire on *attitude, not aptitude*. You can train a person to have the aptitude you will need, but there is no way you can instill the proper attitude. If a person is a winner, optimistic, energetic, pleasant to be with, bright, willing, and on your emotional wavelength, it doesn't matter how much he knows about your company. He can be trained, and he will be a joy to work with, during training and long afterward.

Attitude, not aptitude

If a prospective employee knows your business backward and forward, has ten years experience doing exactly what you want her to do, but has a black cloud floating over her head, sees the negative and is quick to complain about it, doesn't get along with fellow workers, and is on her own wavelength, not yours — stay away from her. No matter how talented she is, you will be unable to prevent her from bringing everyone down — fellow employees, other members of your network, customers, prospects, suppliers, and more. You want your employees or partners to look forward to work. When even one person has a negative attitude and shares it around, you and yours probably won't be too excited about work. To a guerrilla, this represents a failure to achieve one of the most important goals — enjoying the time you spend at work.

As your blood is the life force of your body, needing to be kept healthy with the right foods, right vitamins, right minerals, right fluid intake — your employees and network members form the life force of your business, and they need to be kept in top shape with continuing training, constant feedback, exposure to results, and sharing of your rewards.

In ideal organizations run by guerrilla entrepreneurs, there are no bad employees, no bad attitudes, no lack of training, no self-consciousness at the repetition necessary for proper training, and no hints of amateurism anywhere in their firms. If an em-

No bad employees, no bad attitudes

ployee makes a mistake, he makes it only once. As we cross over from this century to the next, this kind of employee attitude and efficiency will be more valuable than ever.

The best companies in America have what used to be called a corporate culture. This is better described by the term *company chemistry*. The employees have a positive chemistry with the company. So do the suppliers and the independent contractors who work with the company. Having the insight to hire the right people is akin to having the insight to marry the right person. It is more a matter of chemistry than anything else.

I've been married for over forty years to the same woman. We do not have a lot in common, and we knew each other only five months before getting married; two of those months she was away at school. But it was not a difficult decision; it was relatively easy, in fact. And it has not been difficult to stay married. We haven't even been separated, except for occasional trips, for one day.

I tell you this only to show the power of chemistry. That's what we have going for us, and that's why our marriage is working. Although we entered it with a potent underlying feeling of commitment, we never used the word.

The power of chemistry

So it should be with employees for guerrilla entrepreneurs. They must connect with people who have a chemistry that matches theirs. They must find people willing to make a commitment because they want to. They must enjoy being around that person quite a bit, sometimes on weekends, and often during pressure situations.

When I worked at Leo Burnett, then an organization of about three thousand people, I interviewed many aspiring copywriters. After it was determined that they were qualified candidates, I would ask them questions that were not asked by others on their interview trail:

Questions I've asked

* What kind of music do you listen to?
* What's your favorite TV show?
* Who are your favorite male and female movie stars?
* What five words do others use when describing you?

* If you had all the money in the world, what would you do?
* What do you hope to be doing five years from now? Ten years from now?
* What do you do for recreation?
* What's the biggest risk you've ever taken?
* Name five people in life whom you admire—current or past.
* What newspapers and magazines do you read?
* What's the last book you read?
* What's the last movie you saw?
* What's the best book you've read?
* Why do you want to work here?
* Are there any questions I'm not asking, but should be?

These questions told me little about each individual's ability as a writer, but the answers clued me into the chemistry of these people, how they might relate to existing employees. All the people I recommended hiring were hired, moved on to make enormous contributions to the company, and some, alas, later left and started their own firms. I was looking then—and so should you—for kindred guerrilla spirits.

When guerrillas go into business together, they always have the long term in mind. They may be entering into a three-month strategic alliance, a seasonal arrangement, a part-time project, or an internship. Even though the immediate formal relationship may be short-lived, a long-term relationship should be your ultimate goal. With that kind of goal, the need to hire and connect with the right people is crucial.

Your own chemistry

Do you know what all this means to you? It means that you've got to be in close touch with *your own chemistry*. It means you've got to be attuned to what you like, what makes you tick, what motivates you, what brings out the best in you. You've also got to be keenly attuned to your company personality so that you can hire people with the chemistry that easily fits with it. Such a fit should not be a stretch, should not require an effort. It should feel right and natural if it's going to work. If you're not fully at ease with a proposed relationship, that's a sign that you should keep looking for a different one.

Does this mean that you should hire people in your own image? It does not. You should try to hire people who are better than you, smarter than you, faster and more energetic than you. The match must come in the *connection*, not the personalities. Think team, not individuals. You should be able to learn from each other, build upon each other's efforts, create a synergy. Synergy allows two and two to equal more than four. If you hire or connect with someone exactly like yourself, there will be little synergy, few sparks. Indeed, there might be friction.

When you are different, but compatible, when you share the same goals and have similar attitudes, sparks do fly, and from them creativity and ultimately profits and success arise, too. As Leo Burnett used to say, "When we fight, our clients win."

Guerrillas have learned that the age of the lone wolf entre- *Bye-bye,* preneur is long gone. Creators of enterprise must become con- *lone wolf* nected with others to fill in the company gaps. These might be gaps in their own abilities, in attending to customer needs, anything that stands between the entrepreneur and the ideal vision of her business. The world is loaded with gap fillers, more and more of them each year.

Just today, I helped produce seven thirty-second TV commercials for an auto dealer client. It took six hours of shooting video to accomplish what usually takes seven days. The team that made the commercials consisted of a cable company executive, a freelance director, a freelance cameraman, a freelance lighting person, a freelance prop person, and me, the freelance ad maker. I had never met any of the team except for the executive, and yet the commercials were completed with aplomb. When I complimented the director on the speed and effectiveness of the production day, he said that in two weeks everything would be much faster and more streamlined because he was *going digital.* He would no longer be shooting videotape or film. He would be using computers and bits instead of cameras and atoms. Clearly, the guerrilla constantly strives to improve.

If you had to pick ten traits to look for in anyone with whom you connect, these would be the ones to go for:

1. A dedication to the achievement of your company's goals
2. A pleasant personality that is compatible with yours
3. A fearlessness to learn, especially new technologies
4. A desire to improve, manifested by constant learning
5. An optimism that doesn't burn out
6. An abundant level of physical and mental energy
7. A well-organized life, on and off the job
8. The capacity for enthusiasm that grows to passion
9. A balance in life that makes the person burnout-proof
10. The ability to write and to type

If the people you hire or establish relationships with can live up to these guerrilla standards, you shouldn't care much about their other skills, unless you're a baseball manager and you're hiring a pitcher. You can train them to excel at the job for which you need them. You can't train them in the ten areas I've just listed.

Because the people with whom you work are the real life force of your business, hiring or connecting with them should be considered one of your most important tasks. If you do it right, it will also be one of the most rewarding.

19

Treating Your People the Way
They Deserve to Be Treated

IF YOU'RE GOING to hire or do business with extraordinary people and ask extraordinary things of them, you've got to be prepared to treat them in extraordinary ways.

You must be keenly attuned to their needs: compensation, free time, working conditions, sense of involvement, feeling of status, enjoyment of work, sense of control, and opportunity to grow as you grow. As the best salespeople want to work on commission rather than salary, the best guerrilla employees will want to share in your success if they contribute to it.

One of my favorite guerrillas would give his employees one percent ownership of his company every three years—as a gift. No wonder they worked so long and hard for him. Another example is a man who established from scratch a chain of video stores. He would visit the stores unannounced, armed with a pocketful of $50 bills, and hand one to each employee he saw rendering service that he considered above and beyond what would be typical. As a result, his employees kept dreaming up ways to give exceptional service, and his business continued to boom.

How do employees expect to be treated today? Hilton Hotels conducted a survey in 1995. It concluded that the workaholic is passé, that there is no longer any prestige in putting in a twenty-four-hour day, and that free time is the ultimate status symbol of the 1990s. *What employees want*

Nearly half of the people surveyed said that they would sacrifice a day's pay for an extra day off each week. Another 17 percent were more greedy about time: they said they'd give up a day's pay to get two days more free time. Why is this? One hint is that 21 percent said they don't have time for fun anymore.

Men and women did not feel the same way about making financial sacrifices for free time. Whereas 53 percent of employed women said they'd give up a day's pay for a free day, only 43 percent of working men agreed. Men and women were closer in opinion regarding what to do with free time: 79 percent of the women said spending time with family and friends was an important goal, and 75 percent of the men answered the same way. They were also fairly close on their perspective on money: 57 percent of the women said it was an important goal, and 64 percent of the men said the same. Looking at this another way, 43 percent of the women felt that making money was not an important goal; 36 percent of the men agreed.

During most of the twentieth century, money was unquestionably *the* status symbol in America. As we enter the twenty-first, free time is catching up. Many guerrilla companies have been operating on four-day weeks for several years now. Even more run on a four-and-a-half-day week. The trend is toward freedom over cash.

Cutting down on commuters   Enlightened companies help reduce commuting and time demands on employees by enabling them to work from an "electronic cottage," where they still contribute to the firm, but also enjoy free time. That free time is a huge bonus of online communications and the Internet. And don't underestimate the value of cutting down on the number of commuters. The CEO of Intel recently said, "We face three societal pressures: education, health care, and commuting." By allowing your employees to work from their homes, your business contributes to eliminating this last pressure.

Guerrilla entrepreneurs liberally use videoconferencing, high-speed data transfers, e-mail, and faxing to make the personal computers at home as efficient and useful as those used in the office. These business owners know they can attract better personnel if they empower them with technology and reward them with free time.

If you're to successfully treat your employees as they consciously and unconsciously dream of being treated, you will be generous with your praise, never taking them for granted and realizing that the emotional income they derive from your recognition of them is often worth more than a raise or a bonus. The same is true of peer recognition. People just love it. Don't you?

What to give instead of money

When you bestow your rewards, be certain to do it selectively. Don't give everyone the same rewards, and don't give any rewards to undeserving people. Fair is fair, and in the rewarding of employees, this thought must be paramount.

We're about to enter a new millennium in which employers will respond more sensitively to employee needs. One sign is the increasing number of companies that offer child care on the job—*free* child care. That's only one of a zillion perks that transcend mere salary and are really what employees want—and deserve.

Here are a few of the other things they'd take in place of income:

* A leased new car
* A country club membership
* A title
* A larger office
* A paid holiday
* Access to a company boat, vacation home, or apartment
* An expense account
* New responsibilities
* Extra vacation time
* A glamorous business trip

Successful entrepreneurs of the twenty-first century will make use of these incentives.

When I was hiring people for my own department during my life in corporate America, I would frequently offer a starting salary that was less than what the person asked, along with an automatic raise to more than what they asked—plus a new supervisory responsibility if they were still with the company after six months. This gave me the benefit of being able to work within the salary budget I was given. It also provided me with the certainty that the people had earned their salary and their new responsibility. And they sure appreciated the money and the recognition.

A valuable thing to do

One of the most valuable things you can do for your own company, and for your employees at the same time, is to let your employees in on inside information. It will help them feel that they're part of the group and really involved. It will help them focus on your goals, see how they are contributing to those goals, and participate more actively in your success. When they can see how they fit into the process of succeeding, they will work more effectively to ensure that success.

While they help you attain your goals, you've got to do the same for them. When you hire them, ask about their own goals, what they want out of life, how they view being rewarded. Then you can fashion *your* rewards to meet *their* goals. Each is helping the other succeed. This differs greatly from the usual employer-employee relationship, in which the employee feels connected but not really involved.

Fathers and mothers, sisters and brothers

Guerrillas always keep in mind that their employees are human beings first and employees second. They are fathers or mothers, sisters or brothers, sons or daughters, first. Knowing this enables guerrillas to treat their employees with sensitivity. If someone wants to leave the company to form her own firm, instead of resenting it, the guerrilla tries to form an alliance with the employee. Perhaps she will become a member of the guerrilla's network. Perhaps everyone can continue growing together.

Very big on training

The guerrilla entrepreneur is very big on *training* employees in a wide array of areas. In the Hilton survey mentioned earlier in this chapter, 76 percent of the women and 71 percent of the men said that improving oneself intellectually, emotionally, or physically is very important. That's considerably higher than the 57 percent of women and 74 percent of men who said that making money was important. Do people actually put self-improvement ahead of money?

They do. And so guerrillas help them improve. If you give somebody a raise in salary, it helps them, but if you train that person to be better at what he does, it helps him and it helps you. The more you empower your employees and network members, the more you are empowering your own company.

It's very important to know what all your employees really want. They want to be associated with a *winner*. They figure that they'll win if you win, and guerrilla employers prove them right. Guerrillas also do everything they can to be winners themselves, knowing that everyone wants to work with a winner, be associated with a winner, even do business with a winner. Your job as a guerrilla is to win as a company, helping your network members and employees to win along with you. Winning does wonders for status, prestige, and morale.

20

Duplicating Yourself and Your Top People

GUERRILLAS HAVE A TRICK up their sleeves. It allows them to increase their effectiveness, their time, and their freedom. If they do it right, their businesses can continue to generate profits even after the guerrillas have stopped working. This trick is *the ability to duplicate themselves*, to hire and train employees who can make some or all of their guerrilla instincts.

When you duplicate yourself successfully, you set yourself free. You have discovered or trained another to help you reach your objectives, leaving you free to do what you do the best and like the most. The guerrilla's measurement of success in this area can be summed up in a single question: *is the company benefiting?* If what you do the best and like the most doesn't help the company, you're not in the right business.

Once you have zeroed in on your greatest strengths and talents, you can use delegation and duplication to double your profits without doubling your overhead. You can connect with your best employees or network members and ask them to accomplish what you accomplish while you go ahead doing more of the same. This can enable you to produce twice the output, whether you perform a service or make a product. But it does not mean twice the marketing costs, rents, fees, or other business expenses. It will increase some costs, but the profits can easily cover them. For this reason, guerrillas think in term of duplicating themselves from day one.

You've got to be a master of the arts of duplication and delegation; this mastery begins when you figure out whom to delegate to in the first place. The workforce may be teeming with workers, but it's not teeming with people like you. You are one of a kind, and you've got a lot of skills, talents, abilities, powers, insights, and experience that probably cannot be found all in the same person. It's crucial to find and keep people who possess these guerrilla attributes so that your business can be stable even when you're not around.

Duplicate yourself more than once. Perhaps it will take several people to fill your guerrilla boots. For example, when I took off for a recent holiday, I needed people to cover my many acts. Who would give my guerrilla marketing talks? I had already found a woman who would; she's an electrifying presenter and knows guerrilla marketing inside out, and I've seen her deliver presentations before. Who would edit and produce my newsletter? I knew a man who would, just as he has since 1991, leaving me free to write books, my favorite thing. Who would promote my autumn marketing workshops? My guerrilla partner would, and he'd handle every single detail of each workshop, too, attending to minutiae that should be *my* minutiae, but which he can handle with aplomb. And then, there's my online presence on the Internet. Who would mind *that* store? I had established a strategic alliance with an online expert who would do a superlative job—as he always has. Of course, not every one of my responsibilities could be delegated to another. Only I could write my books.

[margin note: Being more than one person*]*

Guerrillas dare not delegate what cannot be accomplished as well or better by the designated collaborator. I've teamed up with writing partners who, while I was away and after I returned, would write portions of my new guerrilla books as co-authors. These guys are loaded with talent and information; they're brilliant writers and dynamite collaborators, but I know that deep down, they're also near duplicates of myself in their areas of expertise, enabling me to get out the word far more efficiently than I could by myself.

Guerrillas do not duplicate themselves helter-skelter, but instead, take the time to pick the right people. They must duplicate the passion, the dedication, and the excellence they themselves bring to the table. And duplicating is not an easy task. It

[margin note: What to duplicate*]*

requires skill at finding, selecting, and training people, potential duplicates, as well as striking a balance between giving them free rein and monitoring them.

I was working at Leo Burnett Advertising in Chicago when I was tapped to help head up an English Leo Burnett office in London. "Joy to the world!" I thought as I checked with my wife, who took all of four seconds to agree to the transfer. We were ready to move that very weekend—daughter, household belongings, the works. But we didn't move that weekend, or for many weekends thereafter.

When I asked the president of Leo Burnett when I could make the move, he said, "As soon as you've replaced yourself here." With several thousand bright and talented people at the agency, I figured that replacing myself would be a simple chore. Wrong. Not so simple. I talked to virtually everyone in the creative department. Many could conceptualize and write as well or better than me, but the chemistry was lacking between them and the people whom I was supervising and our clients. Or they were perfectionists in a group that didn't have the time to be perfect. Or they were meticulous and slow for a group that was meticulous and fast. It took me three months to replace myself.

Duplicating yourself should begin right *now*. Work with your staff or partners so that all of your responsibilities can be handled by others, so that you can take communications-free holidays without your profits dipping or sail away from the business—on a long sabbatical or by selling it—on a boat that follows the river of another passion, whatever it may be.

In order to duplicate yourself, you've got to know yourself very well. I have a friend who, in his own boat, sailed away from his guerrilla furniture enterprise to a three-year round-the-world voyage. But he once duplicated himself the wrong way, with disastrous consequences. He selected managers for his furniture stores from the ranks of Big Corporate America. These people had the smarts, he reasoned, and the track record. He hired them and then watched as his salespeople in four cities began leaving the firm, one by one. The reason: he had duplicated his

A *duplication error*

abilities, but not his personality. The managers he had hired had an uptight corporate mentality in an organization run by a free-wheeling guy. Never underestimate the power of chemistry.

To best clone yourself, make a detailed list of your daily duties and then divide the list into two—doing and delegating. Because guerrillas should never do what they can delegate, they are free to make their maximum contributions to achieving their goals by using their minds, not their time. Duplicating is a *process* that begins early in the life of a business, and continues as the duplicate duplicates again.

Only a tiny portion of most workers' time is spent doing what the worker does best. The rest is devoted to chores better accomplished by others. The better a guerrilla can duplicate herself and then delegate these chores, the more she will enjoy free time, avoid workaholism, reduce stress, feel contentment, and rake in those profits.

To test your delegating ability, take a holiday. See what work falls into the cracks, doesn't get done correctly, is completed late, or comes out substandard. It takes courage to take that holiday, knowing what havoc may ensue. But it takes idiocy and an inflated ego to avoid testing your duplicating and delegating skills. Many people fear that if they delegate, they will make themselves superfluous. But guerrillas *want* to make themselves superfluous. They know they will always find things to do that will propel the company forward, and they discover ways to free themselves to be the creative force behind helping their companies prosper.

Take a holiday

A guerrilla buddy of mine, twenty years a retailer, recently returned from two weeks in New Zealand. When I asked how his business fared during his absence, he answered by telling me that both weeks broke the previous record for sales. Either he's a gold medal delegator or he ought to spend less time at the business.

Guerrillas are interested in duplicating results, objectives, output. And that is just what they delegate to others—the expectation of specific results, objectives to be fulfilled along with the tools to fulfill them, and an agreed-upon output.

In finding people to serve as your own duplicates, here are ten hints that will help you delegate with confidence:

1. Look for people who have *track records*. It's all well and good if a prospective clone is skilled, trained, and says the right things, but if they've actually done what you want them to do for you, and if they've done it well, they should have an inside track in the duplication sweepstakes.

2. Do your *own personnel research*. If there's any data you do *not* want to receive secondhand or by hearsay, find it yourself. Such a matter should not come to you through a filter, but through your own eyes, ears, and observations.

3. Duplicate yourself with *ordinary people*, but train them for *extraordinary results*. Your duplicates can achieve the extraordinary with the right training, the right attitude, the right level of enthusiasm, and by good example. Still, don't clone a mouse to do an elephant's work.

4. Realize that delegating is the *cheapest form of manufacturing*. Guerrillas don't want to build a factory when they can use somebody else's. They know of a curse, quite famous and popular in Italy: "I wish you many employees." You're in business for profit, not power.

5. Try to duplicate yourself through *someone who knows more than you do*. Guerrillas do not feel challenged by a bright employee who might eclipse them. They know that such a duplicate will help grow a business just as long as the person is on the same business wavelength as they are.

6. On the other hand, *someone who is smarter than you* is not necessarily a good duplicate. You've got to take many strengths, other than your I.Q., into consideration. A good track record is better than a great academic record. A pleasant duplicate may be better than a perfectionist duplicate.

7. Look among *your existing employees* to find a potential duplicate. Most employees want to know they can advance to bigger and better positions, so look within to find those who best understand you, your goals, and your business. This helps your business and their morale.

8. Duplicate yourself through people who are *willing to*

work hard. The guerrilla avoids workaholism but does not avoid work. The guerrilla loves work, handles it with passion, and keeps it in balance. Never let pure talent blind you to the need for a hard worker.

9. Creating a duplicate guerrilla is like *getting married.* Think long haul. Take great care. Plan to respect and trust your duplicate. Remember that if it doesn't work out, divorces can be painful and costly.

10. Duplicate yourself through a person who is *not afraid to make decisions.* The inability to make decisions can destroy a company. Your duplicate must be as much a risk-taker as you are. Indecisiveness paralyzes business; the window of opportunity does not remain open indefinitely. If you don't act, your competitor will. Guerrillas would rather make a wrong decision than no decision. Be sure those to whom you delegate work recognize this.

During the twenty-first century, actual cloning of people could become a practical possibility in the laboratory—exact duplication, cell by cell. Until that happens, you're going to have to do that lab work yourself, and your business is your laboratory.

Your business is your laboratory

21

Data — the Currency
of the 21st Century

THE TWO main social classes in the twentieth century were *the rich* and *the poor*. The two main social classes in the twenty-first century will be *the informed* and *the clueless*.

Information will be the guerrilla's ticket to success as well as to

* Happiness
* Wealth
* Power
* Love
* Health
* Longevity
* Security
* Freedom
* Time
* Enlightenment

A scant ten years ago, there just wasn't enough key information for small businesses, and the existing data, sparse as it was, was hard to access. That situation has taken a 180-degree turn, and now there is a superabundance of information, all easier to get than ever — if you know where to look. Online is where to look. The problem then becomes *which information should you access?*

Which information to access

If you were allowed into a vault filled with $100 bills, $50 bills, $20 bills, $10 bills, $5 bills, $1 bills, and pennies, you would know exactly which currency you'd want to take. It would be a simple decision, rapidly made; you'd take the $100s. If the vault was filled with information, clearly labeled, you might not know which pieces you should take. You simply wouldn't recognize the value of each. The crisp green bills might be worth less than the dulled pennies.

Unless you know which information *you need,* you may operate your life and your business based on useless information. To avoid this, guerrillas seek a *data filter.* They're keenly aware that data is crucial for the care and feeding of current customers, for the obtaining of new customers, and for outpacing the competition—which is no slouch when it comes to getting information. Simplified technology and burgeoning data banks offer oceans of data to those who seek it.

New generations, raised on Nintendo and video arcades, now use the Internet as their primary source of data. Intimacy with the Internet is your ticket to ride first class in the information age. Point, click, and be informed quick.

Intimacy with the Internet

Guerrillas wake up, walk into their office, switch on their computers, and hear a message startlingly similar to this one: "Hi. I read 24,394 news stories from around the world this morning. Here are the five you will most want to read." That's what I mean by a data filter. The technology is here right now and has been for several years. Some information hounds refer to it as "broadcatching."

"Broadcatching"

Filtering data is a mandatory skill for the coming millennium. Fortunately, it doesn't take much time if you have datafiltering technology, a computer, and software that lets you program in your range of interests and the data you wish to collect. If your computer doesn't do this task for you, it would take far too much time for you to find and filter data yourself, and so you'll drift backward in time and in accomplishment, impoverished of information, a data pauper destined for the plight of the clueless—watching someone half your age build a company twice the size of yours in a fourth of the time it took you, while you read how she did it in the paper, thinking, "I didn't know those things were possible."

For this reason, one of the fastest growth areas in the computer industry is in helping people find information—aiding them in making their way in a complicated online world, de-mystifying the jargon of computer nerds, and putting the goods in plain view so any guerrilla can access it.

Don't think that the world has already passed you by if you can't access information and filter it down to an amount you can handle. Actually, the world is *in the process of passing you by*, but there's still time to climb on the information and communications superhighway, still time for you to snuggle up to things technical and realize that user manuals are much easier to read than ever. Before century twenty-one makes its debut, user manuals will probably be things of the past because technology will have made itself so user-simple that even the mention of user manuals will trigger a migraine. Nicholas Negroponte, in his brave, brash, on-the-mark book *Being Digital*, predicts that you won't even have to send in a warranty card when you purchase a new appliance; it will be sent in for you electronically after thirty days.

There's still time

Long before the wired Negroponte wrote his book, the technology of which he wrote was hinted at by biz whiz Peter Drucker in 1968. Drucker said, "There is no technical reason why someone like Sears Roebuck should not come out tomorrow with an appliance selling for less than a TV set, capable of being plugged in wherever there is electricity, and giving immediate access to all information needed for schoolwork from first grade through college."

Instead of viewing the information highway as a highway, visualize it as an enormous library that is already built, that delivers information right to your home or office, that never levies late charges, that has both books and ways to interact with millions of people worldwide who know of the library, that operates 24 hours a day for 365 days of the year, that grows and gets better almost every day, and that offers interested parties a whole lot more than information. As one expert has said, "This isn't the information superhighway; it's the information super-library."

An enormous library

The offerings of the major online services today are formidable, so extensive and rapidly growing that to make a complete listing would be like catching smoke. All the services have encyclopedias, and several have more than one. Each has a gateway to even more information and many services to help you find and filter that information.

Almost all the data you access online can be downloaded, printed, and saved or shared. And information doesn't come from only the Internet libraries, but also from bulletin board services, chat groups, and the entire Internet. In many cases, you can merely ask a question, and the online service will provide you with a vast array of online research tools that will lead to the answers. Search vehicles on the Internet scan the world's storehouse of information and put it right up there on your computer screen, ready to be absorbed, filed, tossed, or sent on. The information superlibrary is already at your fingertips, the best location in town.

As information grows more plentiful and accessible, it is also becoming a bit more difficult to define. The distinctions between information and entertainment, software and hardware, product and distribution are fading fast, says the *New York Times*.

Information and entertainment

The guerrilla entrepreneur is unlike others in that she *knows the information that she wants*, and she knows the best format for that information. She also faces up to the difference between information and entertainment and doesn't kid herself, never mistaking her business for show business. She sees the two combined in a new learning form called "edutainment." And she knows that Picasso didn't think much of computers. The great artist said that all they could come up with were the right answers and that the important things were the questions.

If you're beginning to realize that you've got to get digital, to go online in order to be in the realm of the informed, you're facing in the right direction. Cyberspace is the world's largest library, offering you for free, or for a few bucks, information that used to cost a bundle. It will turn you on to new international markets and suppliers, to new business or economic trends, to what your customers are saying about you behind your back, to what your competition is up to.

As a guerrilla, you'll act on that information lightning fast, much faster than the behemoths who are your competition. And just what *kind* of information will you be after?

* *Reports and statistics* that help you understand markets
* *Customer contacts* that expand your customer list
* *Supplier contacts* that help you lower your costs
* *Inside intelligence* and insights about your competitors and yourself
* *Professional advice* about any aspect of your business

But don't end your information search with your forays onto the Internet. True, it's a big library, but there's a lot of data it does not provide, and when information is currency, you want all the data you can get. Some of the information you'll want and may not find online includes:

* Information about your *own product or service*—the more the better
* Information about *your customers*—get as much as possible
* Information about your *competitive advantages*, which you find or create
* Information about your *competitors*, gleaned only by personal effort
* Information about *potential marketing partners* or strategic alliances

In the information age, the guerrilla collects data on and off the Internet, with and without a computer, always blending hard, cold information with human observation and understanding, never viewing the technology as a master, but only as a guide.

So, along with the high-tech Internet, you've got to get information from low-tech customer questionnaires, asking the questions that computers can't ask, that the Internet doesn't ask, that your competitors don't think of asking. Find out where people heard of you, why they buy from you, who they perceive as your competitors, what they like about you, what they like about your competitors, what they dislike about you, the best things about you, the worst things about you, where they'd expect you to market, what they read, what they view, and how you can improve.

These vital nuggets of information won't be found on the Internet. The guerrilla never abandons the hard-to-get information just because other information is so easy to get. Research is the guerrilla's middle name. It's a process, not an event, and it goes on constantly.

Information will help you make money, to be sure. It will also help you make better decisions and fewer mistakes. As a risk-taking guerrilla, you'll do all you can to avoid those mistakes even though they are part of the game. But you'll make fewer errors if you go about things in the right way. As a guerrilla, you are right at home in the information age, and you are committed to remaining a member of the informed class.

Guerrilla entrepreneurs will be their own reference librarians. Because information will be the currency of the twenty-first century, these guerrillas will be wealthy in information before they are wealthy in after-tax income.

22

Getting Cozy with Technology

THE GUERRILLA ENTREPRENEUR knows how to program his VCR in spite of the electronic industry's determination to deter success with an overly technical user manual. He was able to type while in high school and was an acknowledged whiz at computer games. Though neither an engineer nor a nerd, the guerrilla was always one of the first to embrace new technology, showing fascination more than fear and an eagerness to learn.

If the above does not describe you, entrepreneurship may be a bit of an uphill battle for you. The more you embrace technology, the sooner you will learn that it can actually reverse the force of gravity, empowering you to the point that your hard uphill journey becomes a downhill jaunt.

The first key to getting close to technology is overcoming your fear of it. Here we are in a society where $3.3 billion will be spent for online services by 1997, although in 1995, only 10 percent of Americans were online. By the end of 1996, only 16 percent were wired. Why weren't the others rushing to embrace this glorious new way of gaining love, sex, laughs, fun, data, wisdom, friendship, news, convenience, contacts, and profits?

Scared to death They were *scared to death* of the technology.

Most people thought it had everything to do with *computers* rather than *people*. They figured they needed technical training instead of common sense. They thought that if they used a computer incorrectly, they'd break it, or that they would have to go to computer school, take a computer course, or undergo intensive training. Well, at one point in time, they were right. After all, have you ever been able to make heads or tails out of the user manual that came with your cellular phone? Your fax machine? No wonder people were intimidated by technology. You can't blame them for shying away from something that might give them an electric shock or a system crash. They'd heard of the New York blackout. *Somebody* had to be to blame. They didn't want to cause a commotion like that.

But that was then, and this is now. The online services market is increasing by nearly 25 percent a year. Thirty-five million households will be cruising the superhighway by the year 2000, says Jupiter Communications. Why? Because consumers are now more comfortable using computers. They are using them for gaining information, for entertainment, and for word processing, and they're delighted to learn that the world has become a simple place again *in spite of technology.*

Ten years ago, I would have steered you away from much of the technology that I now urge you toward. Not very long ago, I was imploring guerrillas not to "do it yourself" when it came to creating marketing materials, due to their complexity. Now I encourage guerrillas to use the simple new software and user-loving hardware to generate their own newsletters, catalogs, Web sites, stationery, and brochures, to save a bundle of money without making any sacrifices in quality. If there's really an artist in each one of us, technology used to stifle that creative soul. The new, simple technology of today unleashes it, gives it wings, and even assists it on takeoff.

Ten years ago and now

My wife, who used to be baffled at putting a message onto her answering machine, now runs complex art programs on her computer and is designing fabrics on it for a leading fabric design firm. Occasionally, our granddaughter sticks her head in the room and offers her own expertise on the matter. And her expertise is considerable because she is growing up with a computer in her home. I grew up with a piano in mine. That's why I can play the piano, and the only reason why. No lessons. Learning by osmosis. That's what's happening with computers right now. Kids are growing up with them, and society is accepting them as part of the norm. People who can't type are falling behind because they can't avail themselves of the speed and simplicity of e-mail. But more kids than ever are growing up knowing how to type. And they're all cozy with computers. What do you think they were doing all those hours at the game arcade, playing Ping-Pong?

Crossing the freeway

If you want to cross the freeway and remain oblivious to the onrush of traffic, you will have a very small chance of making it across alive. If you want to be an entrepreneur in the twenty-first century and remain oblivious to the onrush of technology, you will have scant chance of making it to your goals.

You will be shortchanging yourself in the areas of time, service, communication, marketing, and effectiveness if you don't leap into the future. It has already started. Forty-five percent of the nearly 30 million computer users in the United States use computers at work and at home. Half of them feel the computer makes them more productive. Why only half? Well, humans being humans, computer users at home also use them for personal correspondence, personal finances, and games. You can't ask a Nintendo champ to quit cold turkey, can you?

The prime benefit of computers

Computers, the epitome of technology and the nerve center of the phone, television, cable, and the human components of a system, bestow *time* as their prime benefit to humankind. Nearly a quarter of computer users say computer use shortens their workday. Computers also give the guerrilla more *flexibility* by enabling him to work anywhere, anytime. It lets him be wired to the office. It lets him be wired to the world. Work-at-home experts Paul and Sarah Edwards used to say computers gave home business owners a competitive edge. Now they say it's the *only* way to be competitive.

Along with computers, getting cozy with technology also means connecting with modems, scanners, fax machines, video cameras, mobile phones, car phones, cordless phones, hands-free phones, pagers, answering machines, voice mail, on-hold marketing, videocassette recorders, universal remote controls, CD/ROMs, and the Internet. Have I left anything out? By the time you read this, I will have.

Do you own a PDA yet? If not, you should think twice about

calling yourself a guerrilla. PDA is the acronym for *personal digital assistant.* Motorola now offers one that enables you to

Do you own a PDA?

* Operate in a wireless mode, with total freedom from wires
* Exchange e-mail without a phone line
* Send faxes
* Connect with the Internet
* Send wireless messages to pagers
* Send or receive messages nationwide without long-distance charges

And the unit doesn't even have an owner's manual; it's that simple. To learn more, you might want to call Motorola at 1-800-894-7353 for a free brochure and the name of the nearest dealer. By the way, that number spells 1-800-8-WIRELESS. It means you should get ready for a wireless world. It's not just coming. It's here.

Guerrillas aren't vexed at when to purchase the technology they'll require. They know exactly what they want to do with the technology they will incorporate into their lives. They've discovered that they should buy the most they can afford. Although computer bargains abound, they buy the latest and the greatest, aiming for the flexibility to upgrade and knowing that the road to obsolescence begins at the door from the store. Today, the cartoon in the morning paper showed the front of a computer store listing a new computer on sale. The store also displayed a sign reading YESTERDAY'S MODEL: 50 PERCENT OFF.

An insight possessed by guerrillas is that *very little really becomes obsolete,* and there is very little to fear. Many advancements in the technical world are minor, cosmetic, superficial, and not even beneficial to a large percentage of people. The basic functions performed by my new computer with all its bells and whistles are identical to those performed by my old computer with no bells or whistles. Guerrillas know their reason for purchasing the new technology is valid, and so it doesn't really matter when the Next Best Thing comes along. Hey, technological progress happens, and guerrillas know it.

Very little becomes obsolete

Investing in technology that is improved upon five months after you invest in it is a small price to pay for advancements such as a quantum leap in computer power—as many experts say, "You can't be too rich, too thin, or have too much computing power." Investing in something that will be improved is a tiny cost for advancements such as pocket-sized computers and lower prices for everything.

Exactly what does technology do for guerrillas?

* A guerrilla in Grand Rapids, Michigan, has no desk at her corporate headquarters, just a mailbox and a phone extension forwarded to her home. From there, she sends e-mail to colleagues and has access to her company database. She has the very definition of a virtual office.

* An advertising agency in Los Angeles and New York City offers all 550 people on its staff the opportunity of working at home, on the road, or at the office. The agency has attracted more new business and had less staff turnover since making the change to the new technology. Says the head guerrilla, "Virtual offices are focused around the resources necessary for people to get their jobs done." That's what technology is all about.

* A guerrilla-run transportation consulting firm that used to pay $60,000 a year to rent office space in Alexandria, Virginia, now is run from the president's home, and her fourteen staff members work from their homes or clients' offices. Quite a reduction of overhead.

What price technology?

Plan on an investment of around $3,000 for the technology—computer, modem, answering device, hands-free phone that you wear like mini-earphones—and a guerrilla entrepreneur can be the professional equivalent of a Fortune 500 corporation. Don't buy anything if you don't understand how to use it. If the technology is not simple enough for you to understand with a salesperson helping you, you're going to be frustrated with the salesperson far away and a toll-free phone number that puts you on perma-hold.

More than 30 million Americans seem to have conquered

their technophobia to the point that they work at home. That number will double by the end of 1998. The reason, stated in true guerrilla entrepreneur fashion by Rohn and Jeri Engh of Osceola, Wisconsin, a home-based newsletter publishing business since 1966: "We wanted to not just make a living but make a life," says Rohn. Adds Jeri, "Technology allows us to juggle work and home life a lot more flexibly than we could ten years ago." They might have added that in 1995, the average adult American earned $25,000 a year, whereas the average home-based business owner earned $51,000—according to The People's Network on TV.

For an example of how the digital revolution will affect the American economy in the twenty-first century, consider that in 1994, Americans sent almost 521 billion document-sized packages by overnight express. The techno-explosion indicates that about 40 percent of that market could disappear as more and more businesses get swept into the digital revolution.

The techno-explosion

How endemic is that explosion right now?

* 98 percent of U.S. homes have at least one radio.
* 96 percent have a color TV.
* 88 percent have a VCR.
* 52 percent have a cordless phone.
* 48 percent have a CD player.
* 35 percent have a personal computer.
* 16 percent have a modem.
* 4 percent have a pager.

I give you these numbers to show how technology had invaded the American home by 1995. The figures will go up dramatically by the end of the century. It takes from ten to twenty years for any new technology, no matter how glorious, to achieve market saturation. But these days, people are embracing technology faster than ever. It's certainly not hard to understand why.

Brian Van Hovel, whom others might consider disabled because he doesn't have control of his hands, has overcome his disability with voice-control technology. Selling computer products from the spare bedroom in his Tucson, Arizona, home since 1990, Van Hovel operates two computers, a laser printer, a fax machine, and four telephone lines merely by talking. As he says, "I speak, and the world turns."

For you to make the world turn, it may take a keystroke, the push of a button, or a click of the mouse.

23

Becoming a Global Presence

AT THE TURN of the twentieth century, business owners were confined to doing business within walking or slow driving distance of their offices. Your more recent ancestors most likely built their businesses in an area within flying distance. Now you can construct your enterprise to do business anywhere in the world. No more time barriers. No more jet lag. Instead of a passport, all you need is a mouse.

Guerrillas know where in the world to do business and what in the world to do to keep it profitable. There is little question that the global market is ready for what you offer. The only question is, are *you* ready to offer it? Right now, five things are happening that ought to spur you to ready your business to go global:

Five reasons to go global

1. There is a slow and steady *merging of multiple national economies* into a handful of huge global economies. This means your target is not as narrow; the bull's-eyes are larger. To boot, these economies want to do business.
2. The cold war is what it should be, a memory, and so markets formerly hidden behind the iron and silk curtains are now opening up left and right. It's as though you were prohibited from engaging in business in a large portion of your city, and suddenly, you're allowed to do business anywhere in town.
3. There is a *slow decline in the standard of living* for millions of people in the United States, corresponding to an increase in the standard in many Far Eastern nations. We are no longer the only game in town. There are other games, other

countries on the rise that want your services. And they are becoming rich enough not to be ignored.

4. There is a *new awareness of time* as our most precious commodity, and businesses with time-based strategies are able to transcend geography. The recognition of time's relationship to inner peace is universal. Technology can free up your time.

5. *Technology is finally becoming simple enough* for both young *and* old to become digital and use computers to enhance their lives. The Internet is connecting everyone to everyone else. Doing business worldwide is becoming more common, more simple, more profitable.

Say hello to the global village

Fortunately, as an American, you will discover that the planet is business-friendly to what you may be offering. American items have built-in appeal throughout the world. Guerrilla Americans are establishing global beachheads as barriers to trade are being rapidly lifted, and as enlightened governments—almost an oxymoron in the twentieth century—enable new and small American businesses to compete in the world market.

Best of all, these businesses are competing on the bases of technology, productivity, innovation, and quality—rather than on price. No wonder exporting has gone up by 83 percent since 1985 and is zooming ever higher as political barriers come tumbling down. U.S. labor costs are forcing a great deal of blue-collar work to move offshore. But blue isn't the only color of money. High-tech jobs are opening up in Europe and Asia at a startling pace, offering global opportunities not only to guerrilla employers, but to employees as well. Marshall McLuhan's global village is here now.

Still, you dare not go global with a product or service you haven't proven in local markets. Only after you're rocking and rolling at home should you think of taking your act on the road. Once you're there, you'll realize that most people don't really care where something is made, even though they do seem to gravitate toward items made in the United States. What they really want is the best product at the best price. If this wasn't the case, you would see only American cars in America.

Guerrillas know that if they are competitive here at home, they can be competitive overseas. They are fully aware that 75 percent of the market for American merchandise is *outside the United States.* And they learn that selling it is not nearly as complicated as they thought it would be. It used to be complicated, but simplification is the order of the day. Streamlined business procedures are becoming the international norm.

Can you realistically hope to take your product to the global market? If it's a good product and you're succeeding with it at home, the odds are in your favor. Great ideas have no geographical boundaries. If it works it Keokuk, there's a good chance it will work in Kuala Lumpur. Maybe it has to be adapted or changed a bit. But humans are humans, and if it's a winner around the corner, it will probably be a winner around the world. *From Keokuk to Kuala Lumpur*

Adapting your product to foreign markets is often as simple as printing user instructions in the language of each country in which you intend to sell it. It can be as complex as adapting the electrical circuitry, changing the size, and redesigning the product. American cars sold in Japan must have steering wheels on the right side. But I'll bet that adapting your product will be a whole lot easier.

Naturally, you've got to understand the culture of the country into which you're trying to sell. Asians place more emphasis on the concept of "face"—that is, avoiding embarrassment—and they treat elders with extra respect, do not use first names, and take care not to call attention to themselves. In striving to understand a culture, guerrillas seek to learn what motivates people in order to grease the skids to the sale. They find that although humans are humans throughout the world, their differences are fascinating. *Insights into Asians*

In England, where I spent three years wondering which century I was in, traditional value is the keystone of business. The British listen politely but are slow to accept new ideas. Here is a typical British response: "I said maybe, and that's final!" *Observations about the British*

Products with high quality and proven value are well received in England, and loyalty is a treasured asset. Although not possible on the Internet, a handshake is taken as a commitment. Truly, the Brits are a civilized group, but frustrating to a fast-moving American entrepreneur lacking in patience. Luckily, guerrilla entrepreneurs are bestowed with an extra dollop of patience — or they'd skip doing business in Great Britain.

Food, wine, clothing, and France

The French are, according to international business author Jack Nadel, hard-working, proud, and stylish. He tells us that loving food, fine wine, and designer clothing is a major asset to doing business in France. As one who did business there for several years, I can heartily concur, but again, I wonder how those traits can be demonstrated online. Perhaps cyber-apéritifs are in our future. A successfully concluded business transaction in France is almost always celebrated with a fine meal and choice conversation. But unlike in England, where a handshake seals the bond, in France it's best to get all agreements confirmed in writing. The reason? Suspicion. The French are terminally suspicious but scrupulously honest.

Smiling in Switzerland

Although a neighbor of France, Switzerland is very different. The Swiss are efficient, neat, and determined. Nadel reminds us that every home, every office, and every factory in Switzerland is as neat as the inside of a Swiss watch. American guerrillas are impressed at the incredible sense of organization apparent in Switzerland. What the Swiss have in organization, they lack in emotionality and humor. Banking is accomplished by the numbers, and depositors are frequently anonymous. But every single thing manufactured in Switzerland is of superb quality and precision. That means keen competition for you, especially if you're in the cuckoo clock biz.

The Italians — elegant but late

The Italians are creative, passionate, and explosively friendly. Doing business with them is like doing business in a grand opera. It is colorful, melodic, exciting, and emotional. Promises are often made without knowing how they will be fulfilled. That's why guerrillas are prepared for the way the final product might arrive — elegant but late.

Guerrillas are aware that Germans believe the only quality

products in the world come from Germany. To a German, the hallmark of quality is to be made in Germany. Like the rest of the world, they have learned that German merchandise is best known for conservative styling and great durability. *Made in Germany— or else*

When operating your business on a global scale, you will be stymied at first by the Japanese, who believe that no decision is too small to be made by a committee. Groups intensely study every aspect of a deal. If you plan to do business with the Japanese, be prepared for a detailed investigation of your background and character. Nadel reminds us that the Japanese would rather enter a relationship than just make a deal. They have a well-earned reputation for finding long-term solutions. If you have the patience to go with the Japanese flow, you will find your reward in loyal, long-term business relationships. *Going with the Japanese flow*

The new Hong Kong will have a major impact on business in China. For years, Hong Kong was the door to business in China. The Chinese bureaucracy has proved a formidable barrier to business because of China's difficulty in relating to a free market and its stifling of creativity. But guerrillas in Hong Kong know how to do business with the West and how to harness the manpower of mainland China. Back in 1976, I authored a book called *Earning Money Without a Job*, which was about being an entrepreneur freed from the structure of a job, about economic freedom. In 1994, the Chinese published a translation of the book. They are obviously headed in the right direction. It's just that their timing is a bit off. *Guerrillas in China*

In Indonesia and Thailand, both of which I visited recently, I was amazed at the people's remarkable willingness to learn, not to mention their ability to understand my language as well as theirs. I sensed a great deal of spirituality in both countries, a coveting of technology, a penchant to laugh and smile a lot. I thought Houston had an entrepreneurial atmosphere, but it's laid-back compared with Jakarta. *Laughing all the way to the bank*

The more you become interested in the notion of going global, the more important it is that you attend your industry's international trade show. Most industries have such shows, and at them you'll find manufacturers, agents, and distributors all under one roof. You can meet with them, see their merchandise, research their pricing, even bounce your plans off them. You'll find that such a trade show is the perfect spawning ground for new contacts and budding relationships in the global market-place.

The language of the guerrilla   The language of the guerrilla (he said with a grin and a sigh of relaxation) is the international language of business—English. Guerrillas never even think about negotiating in a foreign language, no matter how adept they are at speaking or reading it. Nuances in language are often missed by those not born to the language. Sometimes an inflection gives a word a whole new meaning, though inflections are rare on the Internet. The use of an interpreter gives you, certainly, clarity and a wee bit of extra time to think before you have to respond.

Television certainly makes it easier than ever to have global aspirations. Over 1 billion TV sets now populate the globe, a 50 percent rise over the past five years. A cool $65 billion is spent for TV programming worldwide. There are more than three hundred satellite-delivered TV services right now, erasing borders between nations from outer space. CNN is seen in 147 countries, and MTV reaches hundreds of millions of households. The meaning is clear: global advertising is finally a reality. As a guerrilla, you'll keep an eagle eye focused on TV and how it can help you. At the same time, you'll be careful with how you use any of the emerging technologies.

Although more and more businesses are doing business on-line (currently there are 154 nations hooked up to the Internet), and the companies in many nations are making it easier to transact business, Internet guerrillas still use an experienced agent in their forays into global commerce. An independent agent who is a native of the country in which you do business can be a godsend. Pay that person a fee or commission to negotiate for you, check the quality of what you want, and make sure your instructions are followed. Put absolutely everything into writing—even with the British—and get where you're going *before* others get there.

24

Modular Profit Alliances

ALMOST ALL the futurists agree that the rugged individualism of the early days of going it alone, the era of the "cowboy entrepreneur," the one-man enterprise band, is coming to a grinding halt. It is being replaced by what is called "collaborative entrepreneurship." Small businesses are learning to work in networks with larger firms, as buyers and vendors sharing talent, technology, and capital. Collaboration and cooperation are the new foundations for entrepreneurial success.

Guerrillas have known this all along, searching for businesses with which to cooperate rather than compete. It's nice that the world is catching up. The whole idea is to create or hook up with an existing profit alliance. The sole purpose of the alliance is *mutual profit*, and the alliances are temporary, never permanent. They will provide you with small business prosperity—with a little help from your friends. And you have more friends than you may realize. Consider those with whom you might enter into a profit alliance:

Potential alliance partners

* *Competitors from far away.* They probably know what works and what doesn't work in their neck of the woods, and they'll gladly share knowledge with you if you've got knowledge to share with them.
* *Competitors from nearby.* They'll see the good sense of sharing the potential rather than battling for it, and they'll like the idea of reducing their marketing costs.
* *Suppliers.* They know that as you grow, they'll grow, too,

and they know that you're good at what you do because they've been working with you for a while and keeping an eye on you.

* *Fellow entrepreneurs.* They've learned that being part of a loose-knit network is a lot better than being out there all alone, and maybe they have the same kind of prospects and customers that you do.
* *Investors.* They'll love the thought of getting rich by your brains, time, and toil, and you've convinced them that your business will succeed, helping them succeed in turn.
* *Lenders.* There is a strong rationale for any bank or other lending institution to help a company it has deemed worthy of a loan.
* *Employees.* This will make them feel more a part of management, will foster their proprietary spirit, and will ensure their emotional connection, a bonus for both of you.
* *Landlords.* You have proved yourself a desirable tenant who is capable of growing a business, and the landlord knows that profitability reflects reliability, a valued asset in a renter.
* *The community.* Your success will enrich it by providing economic stability and by attracting capital and possibly even employment opportunities.
* *Online neighbors.* They are part of your digital neighborhood, know you, have witnessed your growth, and might see you as an opportunity to increase their Internet presence as well as their global reach.

*   *   *

Guerrillas view *all* other businesses as potential partners, as allies, as possible parts of a network that can help in many ways. They realize that consistent success and growth in the twenty-first century will be a hallmark of teams and not single players.

When you open your mind to the idea of connecting with other businesses for the goal of profitability all around—for an alliance might consist of two businesses or fifteen businesses— be aware of what you have to offer, what you need, and what

your potential partners have to offer and need. You can help
each other in at least ten areas:

1. Planning
2. Technology
3. Inventory
4. Management
5. Human beings
6. Customer service
7. Work space
8. Purchasing power
9. Marketing
10. Information sharing

Generally, profit alliances are best entered into by companies that have *the same kind of customers*. This way, each one can refer the customer to another member of the network—all in the best interests of the customer. Although I urge you to enter into alliances with the goal of profitability, your bottom-line goal should be *the good of the customer*. If it is, you'll be better at spotting such alliance possibilities. You'll know that by entering into them, you'll be able to provide better service.

When I began my life as a guerrilla entrepreneur, not knowing quite how to spell either word, let alone knowing the import of the words in this book, I offered my services as an advertising copywriter. As time passed and my sensitivity to client needs became more acute, I began to enlarge my network, my web of
profit alliances.

First, I connected with an *art director*. Then I needed to provide my clients with the services of a *photographer*. In just a brief time, I saw that my clients and I would be better off if I offered the services of a *printer*. It wasn't too long before I recognized the need for a *media buyer*. The ability to provide that service made my clients so happy that I soon also offered the services of a *researcher*. Shortly thereafter, I knew I could do better work if I teamed up with a *television producer*, leading to an alliance with a *production studio* and, almost at the same time, with a *music composer.*

We referred to one another. We recommended one another. We leaned on one another. We shared prospect names with one another. We expanded our own businesses by offering the services of one another. We provided important data to one another. We gained, and our clients gained. I had been running my work-from-home business for less than two years, and already I had eight profit alliances. The characteristics of the alliances were fascinating:

* In no case did any of us ever commit anything to writing. Our alliances were informal. No one ripped off another member of the network.
* Some of the alliances were with individuals (the art director) whereas others were with large companies (the media-buying service).
* Because I was able to attract more business with my new ability to offer expanded services, my income shot up dramatically. Yet I didn't have to give one penny to any other members.
* I was able to direct gobs of business to my partners and give them new customers and clients without their having to invest one cent in marketing or give one cent to me.
* Some of the alliances evaporated as my partners grew large and raised their fees, whereas some of the alliances still continue today.

I entered into my profit alliances and enjoyed the benefits in a manner that fit my needs at the time. As large and small businesses form alliances at this time, they go about their connecting in a different manner—one that fits *their* needs. There are no rules in this game. You get to make them up, and your guiding force should be your own sense of comfort and security.

No rules

Perhaps you will want to put all agreements in writing, to formalize your alliance. There's nothing wrong with that. Even though I didn't insist on committing agreements to paper, I suggest that you do—because I'm smarter now. Maybe you'll choose to pay your partners for business you get as a result of working with them, and you'll collect a slice of profits they receive as a result of working with you. You might connect with a Fortune 500 company; increasing numbers of them are forming profit alliances with new small businesses. You may even share office space with them, if such an arrangement suits your needs.

These alliances are being formed by high-profile big businesses as well as by the little guys who want the profits, but not the headaches, of big businesses. On the largest scale, you see a profit alliance when you view a McDonald's TV commercial that transforms itself into a Coca-Cola commercial midway through and then ends up as a commercial for the latest Disney movie. You see a profit alliance on a tiny scale when you eat at a local restaurant and see on display — and for sale — the paintings of a local artist.

The guerrilla entrepreneur takes seriously the idea of joining a network or even five networks to test the waters of profit alliances and then to achieve the goals of the business with the invaluable aid of the alliances. Perhaps the business owner will learn that the more alliances, the better. Or maybe she'll determine that one strategic alliance with the right company is enough. I know a restaurateur who formed a profit alliance with a company specializing in the home delivery of restaurant meals. When I asked if the restaurant owner was interested in offering delivery by means of an online service, she said, "I've got all the business I can possibly handle because of Room Service, those delivery guys. Any more and my employees will quit because they're overworked." Okay.

You are in your business at the cresting of the wave of working from home and being a entrepreneur, so you get to set the rules of the game to fit your own tastes. Although Thomas Edison formed a dynamite profit alliance with Corning Glass a long time ago, resulting in the light bulb — electrical filaments by Edison, glass by Corning — the concept of such teaming up is still relatively new. So you can create and mold your alliances any way you see fit.

*No unsavory
characters*

Be sure you don't team up with unsavory characters, with people whose spurious methods of doing business can undo all the good things you have done to establish an unblemished reputation. Investigate your potential partners by asking others about them, and factor in their personalities while you assess their past marketing activities. Chemistry counts.

The task of the guerrilla in the coming millennium will be to spot potential alliances and then convince other business owners to enter such partnerships. When some business owners hear the word *partner*, they think in terms of permanent disasters. Your job is to get them to think not of long marriage, but of a hot affair. For both of you, the thing to do is to *test your idea* for the alliance. If it fails, you've lost hardly anything but some time. If it works, you've taken the first step up a ladder that leads to entrepreneurial joy.

PART IV

The Secrets

To MANY, the secrets of succeeding in the life of a guerrilla entrepreneur aren't really secrets at all, but plain and simple common sense. But because common sense is so uncommon these days, you'd think it is a secret, for so many business owners lack it.

It should be no secret that the key to survival and prosperity is proper management. If everything is in order except the management, expect dire results. If you don't realize that behind all the complexities of business are human beings, you will be lost in a capitalistic wilderness. If changes throw you for a loop and you haven't prepared for them, you should be minding someone else's business and not your own, taking orders instead of giving them.

Comfort with marketing is another secret, since so many business owners are intimidated by it. Because they are, they don't do it. Not a good idea. Marketing involves taking risks that most people don't want to take. To some, that's like taking a risk involving rocket science. Their crash-and-burn mentality dominates their takeoff-and-soar potential.

The way of the guerrilla involves combining the best of the past with the best of the present. The idea of convenience is not very new, but the concept of moving beyond convenience is so novel, most entrepreneurs haven't a clue what it means. It means being the most convenient, the fastest, the simplest company to buy from, giving more than is expected.

A secret of success, now more than ever, is being able to snuggle up to technology so you can be interactive. Interactivity has as much to do with computers as trumpet playing has to do with brass. The computer is only a tool; *people* are connected to computers at both ends.

Sadly, one of the biggest secrets is how to avoid overworking. It may be one of the most important of all, but it is no secret to guerrillas. The other secrets are meaningless if you are unable to provide balance in your life.

25

Managing in the New Reality

SAVVY VENTURE CAPITALISTS look first to the management of a firm before deciding whether or not to invest money in that company. This is not to say that you should think in terms of attracting venture capital with your strong management, but instead, in terms of generating profit capital with that management. Although management can refer to anyone in charge—top level or middle level, duplicates of yourself or employees to whom you delegate responsibility—as a guerrilla, management usually means yourself.

The number one cause of business failure in the United States and elsewhere is *poor management*. I'll bet you're not surprised. What are the traits of good management?

The traits of good management

1. *The ability to focus*—never losing sight of the goal of the business
2. *The ability to lead*—which means to inspire effectiveness
3. *The ability to relate*—to employees, partners, customers, suppliers
4. *The ability to change*—static leadership is doomed from the start
5. *The ability to reflect*—seeing the whole picture

Guerrilla managers lead by *shared values* rather than by fear. They are up-to-date on state-of-the-moment business technology, have the empathy to enjoy smooth employee and network relations, understand the principles of financial leverage, have attained a high zone of comfort in the world of marketing, and are pleasant to work with, do business with, sell to, and buy from. Such traits aren't uncommon among a whole management team, but they are less often found all in one person. As a guerrilla looking toward the next century of success, you must possess these characteristics.

They differ from the traits of the successful entrepreneur of yesterday. The rules have changed, and business reality is different. What worked in the past doesn't necessarily work today— for today is the future. People have different goals, different ideals, different expectations. Management by the iron fist doesn't cut it anymore. And yet, a certain strength in managers is necessary. They are expected to be decisive, to have a point of view, to operate without fear. They must keep their eye on the bottom line but realize that humanity is now part of the equation for success.

Unclench that iron fist

The successful guerrilla managers of today are aware that the hallmark of the 1970s was quality; of the 1980s, service; of the 1990s, flexibility; and of the first decade of the next century, innovation. Successful guerrillas will operate in a structure that is loosely knit, ad hoc, and ever changing, and that has many open lines of communication.

They have learned to adjust to the entrepreneurial initiatives and redirection that characterize working in uncharted territory, where much of the work of the present is carried on. Above all, guerrillas are motivated and driven by *results*. They have learned to measure and reward efforts and successes. And they wouldn't dream of punishing any failed experimenters who stumbled in the quest for innovation and success.

Don't give customers what they expect

Do guerrilla managers give customers absolutely everything they expect? Of course not. Anyone can do that. Guerrillas manage by giving customers the unexpected—which is *more* than they anticipated, *better* than they anticipated, *faster* than they anticipated, *more convenient* than they anticipated, and *offered with better service* than they anticipated.

I just bought a new car last week. The dealer told me it would take six weeks before the car would be delivered. I said this would be no problem. I also mentioned that my wife and I were taking a two-hundred-mile trip the next day to pick out a puppy. Out of nowhere, even though my purchase of the new car had been consummated, the dealer offered me the loan of a new car to take the trip. I hadn't asked. I certainly didn't expect the offer. But I did take her up on it. When I talked about my new car to my friends, I added the part about the free loaner from thin air. You probably won't be surprised that my friends were far more impressed by the dealer's spontaneous generosity than by the new car itself.

The guerrilla manager knows he cannot raise prices in lock-step with higher costs because customers want lower costs, and the competition is able to offer them. That same manager knows that today's customers expect and refuse to settle for less than service that is flawless, instantaneous, and rendered with a smile. Premium service is becoming the norm, and guerrilla managers are leading the way. As they lead, they raise their own standards, making it harder than ever to follow.

New rules for managing

Guerrilla managers know that great marketing can't sell a poor product, so they make no compromises on quality and build into their offerings a recognizable superiority along with dazzling innovation.

According to *The Discipline of Market Leaders,* by Michael Treacy and Fred Wiersema, top companies are now playing by three new rules:

1. Excellence in One Dimension

Provide the best offering in the marketplace by excelling in a specific dimension of value. It can be style, service, price, technology, convenience, or any of a host of others. Great management does not try to excel in all of these because it's right at the border of impossible. They do try to be the best in one of them.

2. High Standards

Maintain threshold standards on the other dimensions of value. Just because you're proficient at one thing doesn't mean you can ignore the others. Ask Yugo, which learned that price was not enough. People wanted performance, too. Or ask Apple, which learned that performance isn't enough if the price is too high.

That's why Nike looks over one shoulder at Reebok, which competes on quality, and at Wal-Mart, a tough competitor in the arena of price.

3. Improved Value

Dominate your market by improving your value every year. You can be sure that if you're doing enough to be a leader, your competitors will be paying close attention, so you've got to continue getting better all the time. That's what your customers are hoping for. Guerrillas strive to constantly deliver the best performance in their selected dimension of value.

While guerrillas are concentrating upon providing the optimum value, the management of the future must be obsessed with helping to understand exactly what is needed, for the guerrilla always tries to sell what the customer *needs* instead of what the customer *wants*. He makes it a point to learn the difference. The guerrilla manager is superb at delegating, if not to employees, then to partners and other members of the network. Decision making is always delegated to people who are close to the customer so that people don't have to check with management before proceeding.

Playing favorites
Guerrilla managers always *play favorites*. They have divided their prospects and their customers into A-lists and B-lists. A-list customers spend more, make repeat purchases, refer more often, and respond to new offers. Those on the A-list receive A-plus attention, nurturing, favors, and service. B-list customers haven't yet demonstrated loyalty, don't yet make purchases that have an impact on the bottom line, and haven't started referring new business. Those on the B-list are well cared for, but not lavished with overvalues.

A common mindset in any guerrilla management is focused on solving problems rather than providing benefits. That mindset is geared to specific rather than general solutions. It reveres lasting client relationships and engages in the care and feeding of customers to keep those relationships warm and close.

I've noticed that guerrilla managers don't go for ostentation or glitz. They don't make a habit of rewarding their employees with cash awards or increased responsibilities. What they do instead is *put people in the limelight*—mention their name in the company newsletter, paste their photo to a plaque, name their best team players as employees of the week, month, or year. Those visible pats on the back do a marvelous job of cultivating a work force. Whether they are employees or network members, that is how to keep your people highly motivated and dedicated to the success of your enterprise.

What kind of people do guerrilla managers look for as work mates? They look for *team players*, for people with the *chemistry* to fit in, for *optimists* who see the silver lining instead of the dark cloud, for people *who can write*, for people who *enjoy other people*, for coworkers who are *a pleasure to be with*, and for folks who are *trainable*. You can't train a person to develop a pleasing personality, but you might be able to train a person with a pleasing personality to be a crackerjack salesperson. *The people guerrillas look for*

What kind of people do guerrilla managers avoid as work mates? *Free spirits*, for one. They may be a joy to be around socially, but they are rarely members of winning teams. Guerrillas also avoid people who can't *sweat the details*, who go to pieces at *deadlines*, who can't accomplish their work within *prescribed hours*, who have *egos* that get in the way of their performance, who are *terrified* of making decisions. *The people guerrillas avoid*

Managing really comes down to locating, motivating, growing, guiding, and holding on to talent. It means choosing people who demonstrate a combination of humility, creativity, and versatility, not to mention a deep and fervent love of learning.

If you were to compile an all-star team of guerrilla managers, the team would engage in these ten practices:

1. They would indoctrinate members of the team in accountability.
2. They would reward actions that are beyond the call of duty.
3. They would commend employees for formal customer compliments.

4. They would back their employees' decisions when talking with customers.
5. They would route customer feedback to appropriate employees.
6. They would have regular company functions to promote teamwork.
7. They would route errors and problems to the employees causing them.
8. They would frequently appraise individual performances.
9. They would make a public spectacle out of outstanding performances.
10. They would not hesitate to fire a person if they had just cause.

As a result of these practices, a guerrilla's employees would understand the scope of their personal responsibilities and the importance of all their interactions with outsiders, and they would take pride in their work and their professionalism.

The traits of a good boss

Certain obvious characteristics mark an ideal guerrilla manager. Not by coincidence, they are exactly the same as the results of an employee poll that defined the traits of a good boss:

* Considerate
* Fair
* Honest
* Just
* Caring
* Impartial
* Communicative
* Interested
* Calm
* Friendly
* Available
* Consistent
* Trusting

You will soon learn, if you haven't already, that managing means taking responsibility. As in golf, where you have only yourself to blame or praise, and unlike the team sports, management is a game in which you are really the person in whom resides *sole responsibility*. When a football team draws a lot of penalties, I blame the coach for lack of good and disciplined instruction. When they make several miracle plays in the fourth quarter to win the game, I give the credit to the coach. Other players may have made the mistakes or the big plays, and yet it is the coach—the guy where the buck stops—who is, in the end, the person who made it happen, or not happen. *Somebody* has to be in charge. And in a business that somebody is the management. You.

Guerrilla entrepreneurs know deep inside that being the person in charge is fun. That fun is balanced by danger. It is also exhilarating. That exhilaration is balanced by fear. It is also rewarding. That sense of being rewarded is tempered by loneliness. It is energized by facing and then surmounting challenges. The best managers have to deal with many emotions, and at the same time accomplish these goals. *Fun and danger*

* They inspire people to perform above their capabilities.
* They create confidence among their customers and employees.
* They are obsessed with quality.
* They have the intestinal fortitude to get the job done—no matter what.
* They have an equal blend of heart and brains. They also have soul.
* They lead by example.
* They willingly take responsibility for everything.
* They accept neither praise nor money if it is not deserved.
* They are honest with themselves and with others.
* They love people.

*   *   *

Good managers love people. They are also aggressive. This is because they are oriented to results. They don't mind bruising an ego or two, but they mean nothing personal by it because their assertiveness is always directed at ideas and not at people.

They are fully aware that an aggressive spirit, a guerrilla trait if ever there was one, is a necessary catalyst in the chemistry of motivation.

Guerrilla management today means paying attention to the needs of those who work with you so that they will, in turn, pay more attention to the needs of the customer—not to your own needs. This will create a perceptible difference between you and your competition. And that difference will be what makes you a guerrilla.

26

Selling with the Secrets of
Human Behavior

THE MORE YOU UNDERSTAND psychology and a few invaluable rules of human behavior, the easier it will be for your dreams to become reality. Most people's conscious dreams are ultimately about *money or love*—or things that can give them money or love. Psychologists who came after Freud, the father of the theory that sex is the basic underlying human motivator, theorized that instead of sex it might be power—or security. Money seems to boil down to security and power. Love actually consists of security and sex, among other things.

The human mind, comprised as it is of 90 percent unconscious thinking and 10 percent conscious thinking, is far too complex to be predictable. Nonetheless, generalizations can be made. Guerrillas make them because psychology is slowly being transformed from a body of theories to an actual science with a body of laws—and because proceeding according to science, soft though it still may be, beats the pants off guesswork or gut reaction.

The guerrilla entrepreneur is not surprised to find that people often make purchases primarily because of emotion. You might think it's because of rational behavior, but that's just not true. People buy with *emotion* and then justify their purchase with *logic*. Left-brained people's lives are ruled by logical, sequential reasoning. You'd figure they would make purchase decisions based upon logic, but they don't. When it comes to buying things, they're a lot like the right-brained people who are guided by emotional, instinctive reactions.

People buy with emotion

All people process their purchase decisions in their *un-conscious mind,* not the conscious mind, though it was once thought otherwise. They may speak using the conscious mind, forming the right sentences and coming up with solid reasons for their purchase behavior. But believe you me, they mulled over the purchase in their inner, deeper mind. Guerrillas know how to access that part of the mind. They have the key to the human unconscious.

The key is *repetition.* Now, put those two facts together— people make purchase decisions with their unconscious mind, and you can access the unconscious mind by repeating your product's or service's name and benefits—and suddenly you

The psychology of marketing

have an idea of the *psychology of marketing.* Selling to people may seem to be a single *event.* But it's not. Instead, it's a *process.* And if you understand that this process involves emotions, you're well on your way toward having the insight of the guerrilla.

To which emotions do guerrillas appeal?

To which emotions should guerrillas appeal to when trying to make a sale? There is a long list, and it varies according to the customer. If you take the idea of success seriously, you'll do everything in your power to learn exactly which emotions are the hot buttons for each customer. You learn this by asking questions, by listening carefully to the answers, by reading body language, by not being in a hurry, and by being ultrasensitive to the needs of your customer as well as that customer's emotional makeup.

The following ten emotions add the most force to a sales or a marketing effort:

* *Achievement.* By owning your product, the customer demonstrates to the world that she has accomplished something notable in her life. Your product or service becomes part of the customer's identity.
* *Pride of ownership.* Many people pay more attention to the pride they'll feel if they purchase a product than to the features and benefits that you offer.

* *Security.* This blanket emotion includes money, love, acceptance, power, and control. Emphasize it if you can offer it.
* *Self-improvement.* We are really a nation of self-improvers; self-help books, courses, and seminars prove to be big sellers. If a product helps improve a customer's life, let him know it.
* *Status.* Everyone knows that any car gets you from point A to point B, but some cars bestow far greater status as you drive to point B.
* *Style.* Guerrillas know that everybody buys style, and the style they buy is the one that fits their own *desired* style, real or imagined.
* *Conformity.* Never underestimate the power of a peer. People hunger to be part of a group, and they often show it with their purchases.
* *Ambition.* This emotion makes people opt for purchases that will help them get more out of life, be it money, love, security, or power.
* *Power.* This unconscious need motivates many purchases because everyone wants control, especially over their own lives.
* *Love.* While working in advertising agencies, I was always told that the happiest possible ending to a TV spot is to show the promise of a marriage. I'm not quite certain how the big spenders — Budweiser, Coke, Nike, McDonald's, General Motors — can offer this emotion, but now you know it. If you can integrate love into your strategy, do it. The Beatles have already told us that it's all we need.

The Beatles as guerrillas

As long as you are using psychology to make more sales, realize that along with emotions, you can appeal to the senses. Aristotle misled us when he narrowed the senses down to five. The good Greek overlooked our sense of humor, sense of imagination, sense of wonder, sense of joy, sense of mystery, sense of pride, sense of sexuality, sense of discovery, and a lot more, but he did give good guideposts to guerrillas.

The best guerrillas appeal to a person's sense of *sight* by saying "That looks great on you." When guerrillas determine that a person has a keen sense of hearing, they're not above saying, "Just listen to that powerful engine." The sense of touch is stimulated by lines such as "Feel the luxury." The sense of smell is awakened by "It has such a clean, fresh aroma." And you can easily appeal to a person's sense of taste by suggesting, "It's so delicious."

As guerrillas strive to learn the secrets of human behavior, *The five nevers* they discover *the five nevers:*

1. *Never make a customer feel inferior.* Customers, like you, love to feel smart. How smart? Just as smart as they think they are. If you undermine this feeling, you're undermining your own efforts.
2. *Never try to impress a customer with industry jargon.* You can use that jargon around bosses, coworkers, even employees, but never customers. Impress your customers with the benefits that your product or service offers them.
3. *Never take existing customers for granted.* They are worth six times as much to you as a new customer because it costs one-sixth as much to sell to them. Guerrillas fervently practice customer reverence.
4. *Never compete with the customer.* It is a game you will lose even if you think you've won. Do you want to win or to sell? You are dealing with customers to help them, not to beat their pants off.
5. *Never try to win an argument with the customer.* Better still, never engage in such an argument. Or you'll win the argument and lose the sale. Remember that there are two guerrilla rules about dealing with customers: first, the customer is always right, and second, if you think the customer is wrong, refer back to the first rule.

Personality types

Both you and your customer have personality types, and the better you know them—your own and your customer's—the better you'll be able to use psychology in making that person a customer for life.

People are either *extroverts or introverts.* Extroverts are talkative, responsive, accessible, encompassing, with broad interests. Introverts are reflective, reserved, private, focused, with deep interests.

People operate *by using sensory information or by intuition.* The sensory ones are realistic, live in the here and now, see things literally, have a concrete perspective, and desire specifics and facts. Those governed by intuition are imaginative, future-oriented, able to see meaning in things, have an abstract perspective, and are comfortable with generalities and ideas.

And then we have the *people who think and those who feel.* The thinkers are objective, tough-minded, fair, critically analytical, and nonpersonal. The feelers, as though you had to be told, are subjective, warm-hearted, kind, promote harmony, and are very personal.

Finally, people can be categorized as *judgers or perceivers.* The judgers are structured, decisive, interested in closure, go by lists and schedules, and operate according to plans. The perceivers are spontaneous, flexible, open-ended, impulsive, and more playful than planful.

You'll need to understand these types as you to *get to know your customer,* to know the real person behind the purchase order or credit card. These psycho-nuggets can help you make crucial distinctions between the different names on your customer list, so that the names remain there forever and ever. You've got to spawn a meaningful relationship with the inside of your customer's head.

There's only one person you should know better than you know your customers. The job of guerrillas is to *know themselves,* though Benjamin Franklin warned us that "there are three things that are very hard: diamonds, steel, and knowing yourself." By knowing yourself, you can know others without imposing your personality upon them; instead, you *merge* with them in a manner that is comfortable, honest, and mutually

Three hard things

effective. To maximize sales effectiveness in the ever-competitive twenty-first century, guerrillas must be able to deal with all personality types regardless of their own personality.

Guerrillas know that people don't like anything to be sold to them. Prospective customers appreciate the attention and the time, but they do not appreciate your attempts to control or pressure them. They do enjoy being presented with the facts so that they can make wise buying decisions, and they like to think that the decision was their decision. They really do want to enjoy a friendly relationship with the salesperson from whom they choose to buy, and if the salesperson is up to snuff, that connection will become a lasting relationship—not a single transaction. Guerrillas also know that people would much rather buy from a problem-solving consultant than from a product-pushing salesperson.

The guerrilla entrepreneur pays very close attention to *people*—individuals who want to be treated as one of a kind. In fact, the most potent talent of a psychologically savvy guerrilla is the ability to make each prospect *feel unique*. This is quite difficult, but it's crucial. In fact, this particular talent will separate the real guerrillas from the wannabe guerrillas. If you learn enough about the prospect, through research or listening, you'll be able to make each prospect feel like a special individual. Don't forget that each one really is.

If you've accomplished that, you're more than halfway home. Most salespeople treat prospects like consumers, like members of demographic or psychographic groups. The guerrilla treats each prospect as though that person was somebody's dad or husband or brother or son. The guerrilla pays close attention to this, lets it come out in conversation, and creates a *human bond* with customers—a bond much stronger than a cold-hearted business bond. The truth is, the stronger the human bond, the stronger the business bond.

The human bond

Alas, it is estimated that only one in twenty salespeople really knows how to use psychology, arouse desire, and appeal to a person's emotions. These are the guerrillas, the highest-paid professionals. They know how to use the client's own words to advance the sale. They are aware of the client's problems because they're such good listeners—so they can position their offering as the solution to those problems, making for a much smoother sale.

Guerrillas are keenly attuned to verbal and nonverbal buying signals—sure signs that a prospect is about to make a purchase. The verbal signals are questions or comments such as the following:

Verbal buying signals

* What colors is this available in?
* How long is the warranty?
* My husband will kill me when I get home!
* What is the cost of supplies for this?
* What financing options are available?
* How soon can I get it?
* When does it go on sale?
* I only wish I could afford it.
* Why is the service so expensive?
* Do you offer credit of any kind?

The nonverbal signals, every bit as powerful as the verbal variety, include the following:

Nonverbal buying signals

* Shifting from being physically tense to being relaxed
* Smiling and looking directly into your eyes
* Repeatedly handling product samples
* Leaning forward toward you or your product
* Unfolding arms that were previously crossed
* Unfolding legs that were previously crossed
* Moving from clenched fists to open palms
* Reaching for a pen or for your order form
* Physically moving toward the use of the product
* Dilating of eye pupils—a sign of acceptance and relaxation

Guerrillas are aware of and alert for these signals. They never pass up a golden opportunity to close a sale or to use the astonishing power of psychology in selling. And they don't limit the application of their psychological expertise to selling. They know they are in the people business, and they know that psychology is a people science.

The way of the guerrilla is directed at the needs, wants, and inner workings of people, yourself included. The more you realize this, the more your life as a guerrilla entrepreneur will be financially and emotionally gratifying.

27

Being Prepared for Change

WHETHER YOU LIKE IT or not, all manner of changes will take place during the life of your company, and many will have a direct effect on your company. Many of the changes are already underway and will continue to develop as time goes on. As a wise man said, "That which does not kill us makes us stronger."

Technology will change, enticing people to work away from large offices. People will change, many of them discovering themselves and opting for more balance in their lives. Tastes and styles will change. The media and travel will change. Entertainment and education will change. Politics and ways of doing business will change. This will create reverberations that will help, hinder, wipe out, or not even make waves for your guerrilla enterprise. It's all up to you and how you deal with change.

The way to deal with change is *to be prepared for it*. This process begins with your acceptance of the inevitability of change and your recognition that your company should be structured to flow with it. The future belongs to those who have the foresight and the guts to welcome it, not ignore it. Most people, unfortunately, do ignore change, hoping it will go away. *The future won't go away* But it won't. It hardly ever does.

These people have great difficulty distinguishing between fads and trends. They pay little attention to changes, expecting them to be temporary, like the CB radio fad of the 1970s, when in reality many of the changes signal trends, such as the growth of the Internet. Fads should be observed carefully, but do not necessarily merit changes within your company. Trends also deserve examination, but also may indicate that you need to alter your company to accommodate them.

How do you tell the difference between a fad and a trend? Only by careful scrutiny. Only with time. There is no hard and fast rule, but guerrillas, with their penchant for constant learning, seem to develop the sensitivity that helps them make the distinction. They are never oblivious to change, never in a rush to incorporate it, but instead are quick to give it a warm welcome and then carefully observe it.

Get ready to embrace change and see it as exciting and challenging, inevitable and positive. You just can't afford to be intimidated or overwhelmed by it. Why do so many people still refuse to use computers? They are threatened and put off by them. Does this mean life is passing most of these people by? It does indeed. Life is like that unless you have achieved a state of peace with the whole concept of change. To help you achieve *Welcome these* the guerrilla peace with change, know and welcome these five *five facts* facts:

1. By 2000, as much as a quarter of all we know and do right now will be obsolete. The life span of new technology is around eighteen months these days.
2. Changes are coming at us at a faster pace than ever before, and one of the biggest is the work at home phenomenon.
3. As you read this, about half of all American families need two paychecks to survive. By 2010, three-quarters will.
4. People entering the work force will change jobs every four years and change careers every decade, because their jobs and careers will vaporize.
5. Women will own over half the country's businesses by the year 2000, but many will be home-based businesses because of the priority of family.

The guerrilla entrepreneur sees how these changes might have an impact on her business. She knows the crucial importance of recognizing *when* she needs to change and *what* to change at that time. She knows that coworkers must be willing to actually make the changes happen. She knows she must manage and implement the changes.

For many people, these changes lead to a longer workweek and to less sleep. In fact, nonguerrillas work 20 percent more than they did in the 1980s and sleep 20 percent less. These people are failing to use timesaving technologies or to delegate time-consuming work. I'm working less than I did in the 1980s, sleeping more, and earning more. And I'm enjoying my work, sleep, and money far more than I did ten years ago.

The changes I've incorporated into my life include my computer, fax machine, online service, cordless phone, car phone, delegation of more work to fewer people, and willingness to speak to groups about the topics I write about—enriching my life, not to mention my bank account. My commitment to a three-day week and to loving any work I do has not changed, and yet I've gone from being a writer to an author to a content provider. But all along, I've really been a typist. *Not being able to type in the twenty-first century will be like not being able to read in the twentieth century.*

Robert J. Kriegel, in his delightful book *If It Ain't Broke . . . Break It!* (cowritten with Louis Patler), compares change with surfing on the ocean and offers to entrepreneurs the Surfer's Rules:

The Surfer's Rules

* *Passion rules.* The best surfers don't spend lots of time on the beach talking about surfing. They love the water and are out there looking for a wave. They are totally committed to surfing in body, mind, and spirit. Some have bumper stickers that say "passion rules." Guerrillas might sport the same sticker.
* *No dare, no flair.* Top surfers are constantly pushing their limits, trying new moves and going for bigger waves, longer rides, and more control. This also means taking risks, constantly challenging yourself and those around you, and improving everyone in the process. Guerrillas are famed for both their dare and their flair.

* *Expect to wipe out.* Guerrillas know that failed experiments are part of the game, just as surfers know that wipeouts occur about two or three times more often than great rides. The idea is to learn from the wipeouts and realize that if you play it too safe, you won't keep improving.
* *Don't turn your back on the ocean.* The uncertainty and unpredictability of change is exactly the same as that connected with ocean waves. Surfers respect those waves and never take them for granted. Even the world's best surfer can be drowned by a wave or eaten by a shark if he's not paying close attention. *Pay attention.*
* *Keep looking at the horizon.* Just because the wave coming next is a big one and can give you a big ride, notice what is coming next. Change might be bringing in a wave that can give you the ride of a lifetime or can send you crashing down into the sand. Guerrillas keep their eyes open and look in all directions.
* *Move before it moves you.* To catch a wave, you've got to begin moving before it comes to you. If you wait too long, it will pass you by and leave you in the backwash. Entrepreneurs who wait too long before speeding onto the information superhighway may become roadkill.
* *Never surf alone.* Surfers know it's important to have the security of a good backup should an emergency arise. They know that by pooling their knowledge and resources with others, they can get the most from their passion. Surfers, like guerrilla entrepreneurs, get a little help from their friends.

I don't want you to embrace any and all change. You've got to be selective. You've got to keep everything in its proper perspective. New information technologies tend to have strengthened the old technologies by reemphasizing information itself and by demonstrating the various strengths of the various media. CD/ROMs aren't going to eliminate books just as TV didn't eliminate radio and videos didn't replace movies.

When realigning your life to accommodate change, remember

that things don't really and truly become obsolete in a hurry. Change takes time, and changes announced as dramatic are usually barely noticeable. Companies want to sell what they are producing, so they'll announce a minor change, such as a bit more memory in a computer, as a major breakthrough. But it has hardly any impact on most computer users. Still, the pace of change is faster now than ever before.

Just as inevitable as change is hype. Do you know the differ- *Change* ence? It's getting harder each day to distinguish one from the *and hype* other. It has been estimated that nearly three-quarters of the information in your daily newspaper has been *planted* there by a public relations pro, a lobbying group, or a government filter. The stock market prices, weather forecast, and sports scores aren't planted. For the rest of the content in the paper, you need built-in radar to separate the hype from the reality. If you haven't got it, perhaps you should talk to an expert who does.

All change is not unstoppable. It is possible to stop some change within your own company. It happens every day because of the corporate penchant for change-killers. Change-killers *Change-killers* leap up and block change. Here are ten common examples of change-killing statements:

1. It's not in the budget.
2. Nobody here can do the extra work to get it going.
3. It's going to decrease our quarterly numbers.
4. It'll never work.
5. Nobody does it like that now.
6. It's not practical.
7. Things are working the way they are.
8. We've never tried anything like that before.
9. That's never been proved.
10. That's not the way we do things around here.

These statements may not ultimately stop change, but they stop companies from changing—even when change is manda- tory. Change-killers are not only unhealthy, but also they're lethal. Companies that never change don't do nearly as well as those that always change. Sure, there should be some natural resistance to change, to weigh its merits and to avoid following fads; change should never get in the way of the primary commitment of the guerrilla's operation. A change worth making should simplify the attainment of your goals.

One more noble purpose of change is to eradicate complacency. Once some entrepreneurs find themselves established on the track to success, they tend to stop paying attention, to get lazy and sloppy, to take shortcuts. Changes keep you sharp, maintain your alertness, attract your attention, help you use success as a springboard and not as a pedestal.

Kids and change

Guerrillas can learn about change from *children*. Children are always changing the rules, the boundaries, the roles, and the way the games are played. My wife, a child psychotherapist, tells me that kids spend more time creating and re-creating a game than actually playing it. Rather than play by a fixed set of rules, they constantly redesign the game to fit the needs of the situation and their own desires. My poker game is no different. My fellow players and I are always making minor modifications in our poker games, improving them along with our enjoyment of the game. Along the way, we've lost only one player who was appalled at our willingness to make new rules. "Poker is poker!" he would admonish us. That's his rule, not mine. And it shouldn't be yours, either. Poker, like business and life, is almost anything you want it to be.

The CEO of Quad-Graphics Inc., now a $500 million company serving clients such as *Time*, L. L. Bean, *Playboy*, the *Atlantic Monthly*, and *Newsweek*, knew that he could make his company anything he wanted it to be. He wanted it to be profit-

Spectacular changes

able and sensibly run. So he was not afraid to make spectacular changes. Yet changes as dramatic as these haven't hurt his company at all:

* He eliminated the establishing of budgets, using current data and his own computer because he considered them to be a more timely and accurate control than a budget.
* He disdained plans because he considered them to be like firing a cannonball—fine if you're shooting at a stationary

castle, but he thinks the business goals of today are moving targets. And he's right.

* He eliminated his purchasing department, assuming that those who use supplies should be responsible for buying them.
* He let everyone in his organization have contact with the customer, going as far as inviting customers into his plant.
* He completely dismantled his quality control department, believing that you can't inspect quality into something and that everyone should be responsible for quality.
* He junked his company's time clocks, figuring that if you don't trust people to work until the job is done, you shouldn't have hired them in the first place.
* He eliminated as many layers of management as he possibly could, doing away with the hierarchy, believing fervently in teamwork, and knowing he didn't want to build a team among unequals.

While making these monumental changes, the CEO *did not* change his basic character. Guerrillas do not try to be what they are not. They remain true to who they are regardless of the scope or number of changes they make. And they never make changes simply for the sake of change. It is always for the sake of improvement.

That word *balance* keeps springing up for guerrillas. Balance between work and leisure. Balance between doing and delegating. Balance between changing and keeping things the same. Remember that balance incorporates two or more items rather than one. Too many changes are as ill advised as no changes. The guerrilla accepts change as part of life and, instead of resisting or ignoring it, uses it to move forward—the favorite direction of all guerrillas.

28

Marketing with
21st-Century Weapons

ANY BOUND-FOR-GLORY guerrilla marketing attack, in the twentieth-century or the twenty-first century, begins with a battle plan. But you can't have much of a plan if you don't know the weapons at your disposal. First, you must undertake a reconnaissance mission to become an expert on the marketing terrain. Luckily, you can embark upon that mission right in this chapter, and you can learn the most important weapons to market the fruits of your guerrilla enterprise and win the prize of consistent profits.

Guerrilla marketing in the twenty-first century will have much in common with the guerrilla marketing of the twentieth century in that it will still boil down to *one-on-one encounters* — in person, by phone, by mail, by e-mail, or by techno-clerk — in which you deal with one human being and have the chance to make that person a customer for life.

True, you'll have opportunities to market to millions worldwide, but even then, transactions will finally come down to a one-on-one situation. The more you make it feel that way for your customer or client and the more you make life enjoyable and convenient for that person, the more likely that person will come back to buy again. He or she had *better* come back, because your business life depends upon your repeat and referral business.

Turn inward   More and more marketing will begin to turn *inward toward existing customers* instead of the way companies used to market — *outward toward strangers*. Your job will be to cultivate and grow your existing customer base, learn every detail possible about these sweetie pies, become one with their tastes, frustrations, desires, needs and wants, families, favorite sports teams and vacation selections, the newspapers and magazines they read, the TV shows and movies they watch, the radio shows and kinds of music they listen to.

In the twentieth century, you have to create good marketing materials with your drop-dead expertise about your product and your industry. The upcoming century demands that your expertise be in your customers. The better you know them, the better you'll be able to market to them. Am I suggesting that guerrillas get as close to their customers as they do to their mothers? Yes. That's it. Mother Marketing is the best term to describe the guerrilla marketing of the twenty-first century. It means loving your customers, revering them, listening to them very carefully, and then responding to what they have to say. Fulfill their needs. Be sensitive to their wants. They take *very* good care of you—they feed and clothe you. *Mother knows best*

Let others spend and strain trying to talk to these people. Your energies are directed toward *listening* to them. Mother, like customer, knows best—remember?

Are most people trained in this kind of marketing? Is the pope Hindu? Most businesses aren't very good at listening at all.

Guerrilla marketers of the twenty-first century will not only be better at listening, they'll also be better at speaking; and when they speak, they'll speak softly, whispering rather than shouting. The whisper in the ear will be a potent weapon. It may come in the form of an instant message typed in an online chat room, or a handwritten note, or a whisper at a community event. Online chat rooms, handwritten notes, and community events will be among the more powerful marketing weapons of the coming century. Marketing professionals trained in the mass-market weaponry of the twentieth century will be lost in the wilderness of the warm relationships that will abound in the twenty-first century.

Twentieth-century marketers have been trained to get big bangs from big bucks, though the bangs haven't always been big. Marketing professionals of the coming century will be trained in psychology as well as business. Like guerrilla entrepreneurs, they will be fascinated with the power and the process of marketing. They will try to make marketing into a *circle* whenever possible, knowing that marketing begins with their ideas for generating revenue, that marketing embraces all contact by any representative of their company with any member of the public, and that marketing becomes a circle only when they have the security of repeat business and referral customers.

It is interesting to note that the differences between marketing in the twentieth century and marketing in the twenty-first century are almost identical to differences between old-fashioned marketing and guerrilla marketing.

MONEY
* Twentieth-century marketing mandated that you *invest money* in order to do a good job at marketing your business.
* Twenty-first-century marketing mandates that you *invest time, energy, and imagination* in marketing your business.

MARKETING DECISIONS
* Twentieth-century marketing decisions were based on *judgment, intuition,* and *guesswork,* and rarely upon science.
* Twenty-first-century marketing decisions are based as much as possible upon *psychology,* the emerging science of human behavior.

MEASURING STICKS
* Twentieth-century marketing measured the effectiveness of its weapons by *sales, turnover, traffic, response rate, cost per order, and volume.*
* Twenty-first-century marketing measures the effectiveness of its weapons by one yardstick—*profits*—the dear old bottom line.

SIZE OF BUSINESS
* Twentieth-century marketing was geared to *ultralarge businesses* with limitless marketing budgets.
* Twenty-first-century marketing is geared to *small businesses*

—and to start-ups and home-based businesses with *limited marketing budgets.*

NEW VS. EXISTING CUSTOMERS
* Twentieth-century marketing is oriented to *making the sale and then going on to look for new customers.*
* Twenty-first-century marketing is oriented to *making the sale and then practicing fervent devotion to follow-up with existing customers.*

MARKETING MYSTIQUE
* Twentieth-century marketing *enshrouded marketing in a cloak of mystique,* causing many entrepreneurs to be intimidated by it.
* Twenty-first-century marketing removes the cloak, *eliminates the mystique* from marketing and allows entrepreneurs to feel in control of it, to understand it, to feel no sense of intimidation by it.

COMPETITION VS. COOPERATION
* Twentieth-century marketing is based upon *competition,* finding butts to kick, heads to pound, businesses to pulverize.
* Twenty-first-century marketing is based upon *cooperation,* finding businesses of all types with which to form strategic alliances for mutual profit.

SALES VS. RELATIONSHIPS
* Twentieth-century marketing aims at making *sales,* for sales are the keys to the kingdom.
* Twenty-first-century marketing aims at making *relationships* because one-time sales lead only to a temporary high.

MARKETING COMBINATIONS
* Twentieth-century marketing mistakenly believes that *advertising works* when it doesn't, that direct mail works when it doesn't.
* Twenty-first-century marketing correctly believes that advertising doesn't work and direct mail doesn't work, but that

only marketing combinations work, and that when you combine advertising with direct mail, they both work.

MARKETING WEAPONS
* Twentieth-century marketing features *five or ten marketing weapons* and urges business owners to use two or three of them.
* Twenty-first-century marketing features *at least one hundred marketing weapons,* half of them free and many of them available only if you're online. The idea is to use many and then cut that number down based on results. Twenty-five is ideal.

The ten best marketing weapons

Of the one hundred weapons available to you, ten are the most important. Ten should be illuminated forever by a neon sign in your brain; you should incorporate them into your entrepreneurial DNA. Can you make do with only nine of these? You can if you enjoy being in business for laughs and not for money. But if you have even the vaguest interest in money, you'll probably want to utilize all ten:

1. Marketing Plan

Not having one is like entering battle under a commander whose only advice is "Ready! Fire! . . . Aim!" You aren't going to win many battles that way, yet that's the way many are waged. Not yours, though. Your marketing plan has to be only seven sentences long—describing your purpose, primary benefit and competitive advantage, target audiences, marketing weapons, niche, identity, and budget. Don't even think of waging a battle or producing marketing materials without a plan.

2. Passion

You've just got to feel passion, not only for your own business and the benefits it provides, but also for the marketing process, the research you must do, your customers, your fellow networkers, and your opportunities. If you don't honestly feel that passion, you're going to have a lot of trouble generating the enthusiasm your customers and coworkers will feed on. If you don't feel a burning passion, you seriously should consider another line of work.

3. Benefits List

Prepare a written list of the benefits of doing business with you. Those benefits will help you market what you wish to sell. Put a circle around those benefits that are true competitive advantages, for they will become your marketing superstars, the places where those who create your marketing will hang their hats. The longer your benefits list, the more ammunition you will have to win the battle for the customer. Your benefits list is more valuable than money, yet money can't buy it.

4. Community Involvement

People would much rather buy from friends than from strangers, and by making yourself part of the community, you remove yourself from the ranks of strangers. Community involvement really means working so hard for the community on a volunteer basis that people are dazzled by your conscientiousness. Your hard work for your community transcends any words you might put into a brochure or ad, proving beyond a doubt that yours is a business worth patronizing.

5. Fusion Marketing

This extraordinary weapon is certainly not a new one. You can be sure the Minnesota farmers had it in mind when a group of them figured that they might get together on marketing their veggies under the name "Green Giant." Fusion marketing has been called tie-ins, collaborative marketing, and co-marketing. It's based upon a simple idea: "If you scratch my back, I'll scratch yours." And it means guerrillas can increase their marketing exposure without upping their marketing investment. The more you try this weapon, the more you'll thank me for suggesting it. But don't thank me. Thank the big jolly guy in his valley.

6. Follow-Up

Nearly 70 percent of customers lost to American businesses are lost because of apathy after the sale, the seller's "love 'em and leave 'em" attitude. The opposite of apathy is follow-up. Many business owners, destined to fail at their businesses, think that marketing ends once they've made the sale. True-blue guerrillas know that at the sale, real marketing *begins*. They know that few businesses practice sincere follow-up, so they follow up regularly and reverently. They are keenly aware that it costs six times more to sell something to a new customer than to an existing customer, and they experience the beauty and economy of referral business. If you ask a golfer the name of the game, the golfer will say, "Putting." If you ask a guerrilla the name of the game, the guerrilla will say, "Follow-up." And those people are *professionals*.

7. Customer Research

You know by now that information is the currency of the twenty-first century. Of all the data in the universe—covering your marketing, your competition, your media options, your industry, and your locale—by far the most important to you is the data about *your customers*. Where to get it? By asking the customers themselves via questionnaires, in person, any way you can. Data is money. Customers have the data. They will happily give it to you if you only ask for it. So ask for it. Early and often.

8. Online Presence

The first seven weapons of the twenty-first century were alive and kicking in the twentieth century. This one was an infant. But with media fragmenting into special interest magazines, zone area newspapers, regional edition publications, cable and satellite television, selected format radio, and targeted direct mailings, where does everything come together? *Online and right at your Web site*—on the Internet. I realize this is not happening right now, but it will very soon; and when it does, if you're not ready, you'll be in too late. All your marketing will eventually pay off at your Web site. The World Wide Web is still a baby, but it's a baby that you want to have as a very close friend.

9. *The Designated Guerrilla*

Every twenty-first-century business will need one, and if it's not you—because you lack the time or the passion for solid guerrilla marketing—it should either be someone from within your organization who just loves the idea of riding herd over a superabundance of marketing weapons or someone from the outside who feels the same way and understands your mindset. The whole purpose of guerrilla marketing is action. These weapons are meaningless without the infusion of action provided by your designated guerrilla. This book may be opening the door for you, but it's up to you to walk through the doorway.

10. *Satisfied Customers*

Every person you have satisfied in the past is another weapon in your arsenal, another name for your mailing list, another source of repeat business, another person who will refer others to you. Satisfied customers are the wondrous spring from which flow testimonial letters, success stories, referral business, and before-and-after tales. Best of all, this marketing weapon doesn't cost anything. It actually pays.

As a budding guerrilla entrepreneur, you have probably immersed yourself in the giddy joys of guerrilla marketing, but on the off chance that you've been busy reading novels instead, allow me to give you the essence of guerrilla marketing in the twelve-word credo that should be your marketing manifesto for the twenty-first century. Each of the words ends in the letters *ent*. I give you this memory crutch because it's crucial that you memorize, and then live by, these twelve words. After all, I don't want guerrilla entrepreneurs falling on their noses when it comes to *marketing*.

The guerrilla credo

1. *Commitment.* Is there one word that is the secret of what makes marketing work? There is indeed: *commitment.*

2. *Investment.* When you write a check, it feels like an expense; but marketing, done properly, is the best investment possible in America. It gives you a better payoff than bank investments, holds less risk than stock and bond investments, and gives you a return on your investment that is unparalleled — if you do it right. By living by the twelve-word guerrilla credo, you will be doing it right.

3. *Consistent.* It takes people time to notice you, pay attention to you, trust you. If you make too many changes, they'll be unable to trust you. You can change your headlines, offers, prices, and copy, but don't change your identity or your media or visual format.

4. *Confident.* This is the number one reason that customers patronize the businesses they do. Quality is second, service third, selection fourth, and price fifth.

5. *Patient.* This word describes you because only patient people can practice enough commitment to make people confident.

6. *Involvement.* This describes the relationship between you and your customers. Follow-up proves your involvement; repeat sales prove theirs.

7. *Assortment.* Guerrillas realize marketing isn't advertising but a wide assortment of weapons. Start with a lot; end up with the proven ones.

8. *Convenient.* This word for the upcoming century means you're easy to do business with — offering extended days and hours, making payment a snap.

9. *Subsequent.* Here is where the profits come in — subsequent to the sale, and they are sent soaring by your firm adherence to customer follow-up.

10. *Amazement.* There are things you take for granted about your business. But your marketing should feature all the elements that amaze people.

11. *Measurement.* You can double your profits if you carefully keep track of which weapons hit bull's-eyes and which ones miss the target completely.

12. *Dependent.* This word summarizes your relationship with other businesses; you help each other, cooperating and co-marketing.

✻   ✻   ✻

As you read this, the market is busily splintering into fragments. Guerrillas have a name for these fragments. They call them niches. They know that niches are becoming smaller and smaller and that if they select the right niche, they may be more than halfway home already. As niches grow smaller, customers grow more important—and they know it, so you'd better be prepared to give them the treatment they deserve.

Selecting your niche

You'd better be prepared to "narrowcast" instead of broadcast, to do micromarketing instead of mass marketing, to reach inward toward customers more than outward toward prospects. Guerrilla entrepreneurs are gloriously positioned to capitalize on niche marketing. They're able to differentiate themselves in ways important to their prospects and customers. They're able to get rolling on that information and communications highway in a way that little guys couldn't in the mid–twentieth century. Now everyone can afford a computer and online service. Is this the price of admission to the future? You know it is. Does that mean technology will outweigh the human touch? Just the opposite. Personal selling will be more important that ever, and online communication will add the personal element. People today buy from those they trust. People tomorrow will do the same. The two forces that govern sales will be *advanced technology* and *personal service*. Combining them, guerrilla marketers will thrive as never before.

Enjoying the process of marketing and then using it to its greatest advantage are, without question, essential to the way of the guerrilla.

29

Moving Beyond Convenience

UNTIL NOW, many entrepreneurs have had it easy. They have operated their businesses for *their own convenience*, just as they have since the dawn of individual enterprise. In fact, it wasn't until the 1980s that the business world woke up and came to its senses. Business, its managers finally realized, isn't something you run for a seller's convenience, but for a *customer's* convenience. The thought itself was entrepreneurial heresy but proved to be accurate, and soon many businesses began offering their customers more convenience in many ways.

Businesses started by staying open for longer hours and then for extra days. Where they once refused to sell on credit, they came to accept many credit cards. Where they didn't even consider delivery, they realized that if they didn't deliver, they'd suffer from a competitive disadvantage—so they offered delivery.

In some cases, the services were granted grudgingly because the business owners weren't enthralled at staying late, wrapping gifts, or taking phone orders. But in other instances, the services were enthusiastically offered, and the customers were made to feel as though the business owner actually wanted to render the extra service.

Wanting to serve

Guerrilla entrepreneurs recognize that the actual *wanting* to render extra service is the attitude that customers appreciate, that keeps them coming back for more, that is the true way of the guerrilla. An integral art of great service is a *great attitude*.

Because of this crucial realization, guerrillas hire and team up with people who have this attitude, who sincerely want to help rather than helping because it's part of the job. Members of the guerrilla-run organization think in terms of wanting to help, not making people wait, being as responsive as possible, being the easiest business in town to buy from. They view their work not only as offering convenience, but also as moving *beyond* convenience to where doing business with them is a downright pleasure to experience. How can you move beyond convenience? You begin with the right attitude of *wanting to serve,* and then you can embrace these twelve practices as part of the way you do business:

Twelve guerrilla practices

1. You enable prospects and customers to make purchases from you *365 days a year.* The era of the five-day workweek has passed, leaving in its wake all those businesses that thought transactions should take place Monday through Friday only. Remember, customers are usually at work Monday through Friday. Weekends are far more convenient for them. Guerrilla enterprises cater to this need by remaining open for business.

2. You enable prospects and customers to buy from you *twenty-four hours a day.* Catalog companies across America realize this. So does Safeway, 7–11, most banks, and many gas stations. Once again, most people work from nine to five, so the only time they can give their business to you is after—or before—working hours. If you want their business, you're going to have to adjust your working hours. That's what I mean by moving beyond convenience—moving beyond your own convenience and inconveniencing yourself a bit.

3. You accept *as many credit cards* as possible. Many people are up to their credit card limit on their Visa cards and Master-Cards. To nonguerrillas, this means no sale. To guerrillas, this means their customers can pay for a purchase using a Discover card, American Express card, Carte Blanche, a Diner's Club card—anything, just as long as you don't lose money on it. Don't worry about the percentage you must pay the credit card company; its a tiny investment when it comes to pleasing a customer. Anyhow, 6 percent of something means more profits to you than zero percent of nothing. Instead of bemoaning the percentage, realize your customers are applauding the convenience.

4. You offer *flexible financing,* recognizing that folks like

little numbers a lot more than big numbers. Arrange it so that their down payment isn't necessary for a while, so that quick payment is the same as buying for cash, so that payments may be stretched over the period of time that fits the comfort level of your customers. Break that big, hard-to-handle number into twelve or twenty-four smaller, easy-to-handle payments. It used to be that you bought big-ticket items—cars and houses—only with regular payments. Now, many people pay for yearly magazine subscriptions with three payments. *Time* magazine has reaped a subscription bonanza since they began stressing that point.

5. You have a *toll-free telephone number.* This makes it easier for customers to order your products or services. You also use it to handle inquiries, get names of brochure requesters, render service, and track your advertising. It can even double your response rate. If you're dealing with the local community in your own area code, you don't have to offer this convenience. People like to deal with local businesses when possible. But if you're not, your toll-free phone number can offer the economy and convenience of a local call.

6. You produce at least *two catalogs* per year. This helps your customers keep up-to-date on your offerings, gives you top-of-the-mind awareness, reminds customers of your additional selection, and serves as a superb follow-up tool. Catalogs serve as forums for products, services, notes from you, testimonial letters, PR reprints—a lot of things that help you. And all along, catalogs are customer conveniences, giving them instant access to your products and services.

7. Your business forms are *easy to read and understand.* They help advance people to the next sale without intimidating them with business gobbledygook. Rid your enterprise of these clarity obfuscators. By making your business more oriented to people than to business ideas, you make it more accessible and therefore more convenient.

8. Give callers information *while they're on hold.* Being put on hold when you make a call is frustrating and time-consum-

Business gobbledygook

ing. But if you get valuable or entertaining information while you're waiting, much of the sting is removed. Guerrillas turn on-hold time into marketing time by filling it with information to help the customer as a business person and as a human being. Over 85 percent of people will continue listening to your message for as long as three minutes if you make it helpful and interesting.

9. Think in terms of *saving time for your customers*. Examine every aspect of your business and how it relates to your customers. Eliminate any practices that take unnecessary time, any departments or network members that create bottlenecks. Put yourself in your customer's shoes — order what you sell, and then examine the process from the standpoint of your customer. Will you find any ways to speed up the process? My guess is that you will.

10. Get a *fax machine* so that you and your customers can communicate instantly. They are usually in a hurry and will appreciate the opportunity to show you what they're talking about or see what you're talking about, courtesy of the facsimile machine, now endemic to U.S. business.

11. Get an *e-mail address* because everyone and their cousin is getting a computer and a modem and going online. The ultimate in convenient communication, your e-mail will facilitate twenty-four-hour-a-day, seven-day-a-week business transactions, giving the impression that your business is always open. Customers with e-mail will actually resent your not giving them the convenience they have come to appreciate in transactions with other businesses.

12. Do all in your power to *say yes to every customer request.* *Just say yes* The customer will consider it the ultimate in convenience and service. Now I know that you won't be able to answer in the affirmative 100 percent of the time, but if you try as hard as you can, you'll do better than most of your competitors and better than most businesses with which your customers deal. Try to bypass tradition if it helps the customer. If someone asks for delivery because of special circumstances and you don't offer

delivery, deliver to that customer and be glad you had the opportunity to prove your flexibility and reputation for offering convenience.

The coming of a new century makes people receptive to new ideas and alert to innovation. Many small businesses are vying for customer attention and their disposable income. And true guerrillas will make valiant efforts to win the hearts of their customers. But will they move beyond mere profit and loss, paying attention to the *human side* of doing business with them? Will they be aware of the myriad *details* surrounding any transaction—from the decision to purchase to the use of the product?

It is in the human side of doing business and in the details that convenience and inconvenience may be found. After several years of not so gently hinting that we needed new sofas, my wife finally got through to me. I was reading the newspaper when an ad for Macy's caught my eye. Actually, it was an ad for a sofa sale going on at Macy's at just that moment. The sale wasn't the grabber for me. The sofa styles in the pictures caught my fancy. I read the copy. Yes, they were leather. Yes, they came in ivory. Yes, they were available in the right sizes. And yes, they fit our budget.

When Macy's blew it

I discussed it with my wife, and then I called Macy's. "Hello, do you have in stock the sofas pictured in your full-page *San Francisco Chronicle* ad?" I asked. "We sure do" was the happy answer. "Do you have the ivory, and do you have it in the fifty-four-inch width?" "We do." I was delighted. "Do you deliver? I'm right in your area." "Yes" was the answer. I began visualizing the ivory sofas in the living room, just where we'd place them. "Great. I'd like to order them. When you deliver, will you pick up our two old sofas?"

"No."

"No?"

"No. Picking up used furniture is not part of our service."

"Oh, I see. Well, thank you," I said. And I hung up, but only for an instant, because there in front of me was the same *San Francisco Chronicle,* and as I leafed through it during my call to

Macy's, I had discovered a sofa ad by The Leather Factory. I called their number. Getting to the heart of the matter, they had similar sofas of similar sizes at similar prices, and they did deliver. When I asked if they'd pick up the old sofas, the man said, "Of course."

That sale was made strictly on the basis of convenience. The stores are very close to each other, so the sofas were easy to inspect. And almost everything else was the same. Except for the convenience.

Speed and convenience. They're the competitive advantages for the twenty-first century.

30

Getting Interactive

WHAT'S THE FIRST THING to enter your mind when you read the word *interactive?*

Most entrepreneurs think first of technology. Guerrilla entrepreneurs think first of people. Guerrillas know that *interactive* means "to act reciprocally," rather than to act technologically. Being interactive means being connected, giving and taking, responding. Connections that promote interactivity take place in person, by phone, by mail, and online. That means that guerrillas are interactive in a multitude of forums.

The many ways of being interactive
The traditional *sales call* is probably the most widespread method of conducting business interactively. Zero technology is required. Maximum psychological savvy helps. Guerrillas relish the eye contact, the warm handshake, the smell of ink drying on the dotted line. They may not even own a computer but are classic examples of being interactive.

A guerrilla's *involvement with the community* is also a form of interactivity. In this case, the interaction is first with a group and then with individuals. A truly interactive guerrilla is a member of several community organizations, contributing to the betterment of the local scene as well as being in a position to do some powerful *networking*—still another form of interactivity.

Brochures, electronic and printed, are interactive tools because they are requested or mailed; then they provide information before asking for action, usually a purchase. And to promote interactivity, they frequently offer a coupon, a toll-free phone number, or an e-mail address. Interactivity doesn't always require a lot of back-and-forth communication, as you would

experience in face-to-face meetings and phone calls (the ultimate in interactivity). To be interactive, someone acts and someone else reacts. The amount of acting and reacting is irrelevant.
Getting the desired action is all that counts.

Interactive guerrillas also rely upon the power-packed tool
of a *toll-free phone number* to enhance their interactivity—both
outgoing and incoming. Used for outbound telemarketing, the
phone is used to a high degree and to great advantage by businesses that communicate with other businesses. *Telemarketing* is
a more frequently used technique than direct mail because of
the rapport it builds and the speed at which sales can be consummated. Not a lot of people consider it interactivity, but it is
the essence of the beast.

Guerrillas who realize that interactivity leads to lasting relationships with customers are also hitting the interactive trail
when they offer *free consultations*, a potent marketing weapon if
ever there was one, with *free seminars* that invite questions and
are set up to close sales, and with *speakers who talk to groups* for
free and then distribute brochures and establish relationships.

Without question, *trade shows* are bastions of interactivity *Bastions of*
and an enormous volume of transacted business. On the trade *interactivity*
show floor at the *display booth* as well as in the fancy *hospitality
suite*, billions of dollars in business is conducted in face-to-face
meetings.

Direct mail is certainly interactive, asking for action in every
envelope and making it easy for the recipient to buy what is
being sold. The same is true for almost every advertisement with
a coupon and every commercial with a toll-free number. People
use these tools to be interactive, doing all in their power to
motivate action on the part of their prospects.

A relative newcomer to the interactive culture is *fax-on-
demand*, a method by which people can learn of your offering
and then request more information by fax machine. And the fax
machine then becomes an interactive tool, for it provides an
action and invites an interaction.

Radio and TV commercials that feature toll-free numbers are
dabbling seriously in the interactive world. Their aim at obtain-

ing action in the form of a phone call is brought into even sharper focus by *infomercials*, those broadcast-length TV commercials that look like TV shows but are really heavy artillery in the interactive world.

Home shopping TV channels are built entirely on interactivity. Rarely does a moment pass when the toll-free number isn't flashing on the screen. They even televise their interactivity, showing the viewing public (which is growing at a breathtaking rate) the fun and instant gratification that can be enjoyed when you get interactive. They let the public listen in to the excited folks who order on the phone. Perhaps the most seductive device on TV is Home Shopping Network's countdown clock, which warns viewers that they have only a few moments left to buy before an item is gone forever. In true guerrilla fashion, this technique creates a sense of urgency in the viewer.

Cable TV channels are reaching out too, striving to be interactive so that their advertisers can derive the benefits of give and take with large audiences. Some stations make an offer and then allow customers to ask questions and order—using their TV and a remote device supplied by the cable station. Guerrillas are keeping an eagle eye on these interactive TV efforts, knowing that they are still just experiments and that the public will be rather slow to embrace them. Some, if not all, may one day prove successful. At that point, the guerrilla will adopt that practice.

Another influence on guerrilla behavior is *the Internet*. Whatever people read, wherever they look, they keep learning about the Internet. According to the market research firm Odyssey, Internet use doubled between the fall of 1995 and the spring of 1996. Another study said that subscriptions to U.S. online services surged by 64.4 percent in 1995. More rapidly than anyone dreamt possible, Americans are signing up *to be online*, to connect with millions of people around the world, to become interactive in a whole new way. The entire concept of going online, connecting to the Internet, or having a site on the World Wide Web is giving guerrillas a whole new outlook on being interactive. This method uses technology but deals with human beings, not machines.

There are several ways that guerrilla entrepreneurs conduct, market, and transact their business online. Here are the six most common ways.

1. *Online mailing lists* are lists of people who are interested in a particular topic and absolutely love getting e-mail about it. Thousands of mailing lists are available for a price on over a thousand topics, and they offer many advantages. You can communicate solely by e-mail, which is speedy and inexpensive. You can get reactions to your communications sent directly to your e-mail address, so you don't have to search for them. And the names have been narrowed down to a prequalified group of people, the hottest of your hot prospects, because the lists are so specific. Guerrillas have discovered great profitability in using e-mail.

2. *Electronic storefronts* are sites or home pages on the World Wide Web. They give you a location in cyberspace where you can present your story, give additional information, display merchandise, and even take orders. They're the fastest-growing part of the Internet. If you have a brochure, it should be published on your Web site.

3. *Forums and newsgroups* are specific to a certain subject and enable you to post a message, free of charge, and then to check the message board at a later date to find messages responding to yours. There are more than fifteen thousand Internet newsgroups right now, and that number has grown since you started reading this chapter. It isn't proper netiquette (Internet etiquette) to be blatantly commercial in your interaction with newsgroups, but if you become known within them as a source of good data, you can capitalize on your brilliant reputation. One guerrilla is reported to have netted a bit over $3 million in one year by offering his computer operating system expertise online and then rendering it off-line—by phone or in person.

4. *Chat rooms* are online groups of people connected by a

desire to interact. Hundreds of different chat rooms exist at every moment on the Internet, and you can be sure that some of them are discussing something to do with your industry. If you find and become active in that room, carefully avoiding overt commercialism, you could drum up more than a little business, and it won't cost anything but your online charge, under $10 a month, plus a few bucks per hour—and you get several free hours per month before the hourly charge kicks in.

5. *Bulletin board services* allow you to post messages, run free classified ads for your business, and interact with people who have intentionally signed up for that service because they are intrigued by the subject matter. If the subject matches your industry and you can fulfill the needs of the other members, you're in cyber-clover because it won't cost you anything to do your marketing. Some guerrillas start their own bulletin board services centered on topics near and dear to their own hearts—to build their credibility and their sales.

6. A *World Wide Web site* is an online presence you can call your own. It can link you with many other companies and lets them link with you. A Web site allows you to display your items for sale and to include all the information customers could ever want, even giving them a chance to order or ask questions. Web sites enable you to show still photos or video images and also provide ample space for all the text you feel is important for customers and prospects to read. If you've got a brochure, you should seriously consider putting it on the Web. To see the myriad possibilities, just check the Guerrilla Marketing Web site at www.gmarketing.com. Daily I receive online questions from visitors to my site, and I answer them pronto. You should, too. Fast response time is crucial and is the essence of interactivity.

Being interactive means not only giving information, but also seeking information. The Internet allows you to engage in market research—and accomplish this for hardly any investment in an age when information is king.

Informal focus groups on the Internet that include the appropriate people will let you know whether your products or services have flaws or good potential. You can get honest feedback from people just like your prospects. Guerrillas use this capability as disaster avoidance. They make valuable use of the Internet by exploring these focus groups, by perusing the wealth of reference material available, and by subscribing to electronic clipping services. *Disaster avoidance*

The Internet is the fastest-growing method of being interactive. Remember that no matter how large it gets, it will always be about people, will always boil down to one-on-one transactions, and will never replace face-to-face contact. The Internet is faster, more convenient, and far more economical than mass media in reaching large numbers of people. But you should never consider your business to be interactive strictly because you subscribe to an online service or have your own.

How do you answer your phone? If you don't make all callers feel good that they called you, you're dropping the interactive ball. If you keep them on hold without informing or entertaining them, you're falling on your interactive keister. In person, if you don't look them in the eyes when you talk to them, you're not giving interactivity all that you should. If you don't know their names, smile at them when you see them, or know about their personal lives, you're missing out on the most important aspect of interactivity—relating, human to human, as closely and warmly as possible.

Guerrilla entrepreneurs know well that the key part of the word *interactive* is *active*, and they maintain a high degree of action on as many interactive fronts as possible. They put out the word about their offerings and their benefits in as many places as possible, and each time, they invite dialogue and provide their address (e-mail or snail mail), their fax number, and their phone number. One wildly successful guerrilla I know provides his home phone number along with his office number. He says that the few calls this elicits are more than compensated for by the feeling of connection and security that it gives to his clients. He proves his interactivity by making himself available at any hour of any day. *The key word is active*

The chairman of Procter and Gamble, hardly a guerrilla

company but one that knows its business, said in the mid-1990s, "We can't be sure that ad-supported TV programming will have its future in the world being created—a world of video-on-demand, pay-per-view, and subscription TV." The company, as I type this paragraph, spends about 90 percent of its $3 billion advertising budget on television. The new media, observes the esteemed chairman, are designed to carry no advertising at all. So Procter and Gamble is now discussing major interactive entertainment projects with Time-Warner. You would be well advised to learn from this example involving a company that enjoys a market penetration of 97 percent in the United States.

31

Avoiding Workaholism and Stress

IF YOU'RE PLANNING to become a full-scale, full-tilt, high-energy guerrilla entrepreneur, don't forget that one of the commitments you'll be making is a commitment to balance your zeal for making a living with a zest for making a life.

A life dedicated primarily to working and amassing a fortune is only part of a life if friends, family, fun, recreation, and relaxation are left in the dust. Guerrillas are much more than earning machines. Almost anyone focused on money will get it if they put in enough time and effort. Achieving serenity and balance is more difficult. There are fewer role models for this lifestyle. The newspapers list only the one hundred wealthiest people in the world, not the one hundred happiest.

To get your name on the list of the one hundred happiest people, there are five very important things you need to know: *Five important things*

1. Succeeding in your own business means that you must constantly work *more than forty hours a week, weekends, and evenings.*
2. Running your own enterprise carries with it the realization that the responsibilities *will cause stress,* sometimes lethal.
3. There *really is a Santa Claus,* and his sleigh is pulled through the sky by reindeer every Christmas Eve.
4. *The Easter Bunny exists all year long* and spends all of his time as an egg-painting workaholic.
5. The *Brooklyn Bridge actually is for sale* right now, and you can have it for only $10. All credit cards are gleefully accepted.

*Don't believe
a lie*
File those unfacts away where you keep your tales by the Brothers Grimm and your poems by Mother Goose. They are widely believed, but they simply aren't true. The true workaholics are those who choose work over any other method of spending time—a woeful condition. They fail to plan ahead and incorporate balance into their lives, they lose control of situations to extraneous circumstances and spend time putting out fires instead of generating profits, and they have misguided priorities and operate according to early-twentieth-century dictates.

You often read of the problems caused by abuse of alcohol and the depressingly high number of people who die of alcoholism. But you don't see much about abuse of work and the fact that more workaholics are dying faster and younger than alcoholics, that the affliction called "karoshi syndrome"— death from overwork—is now the number two cause of death in Japan.

Diane Fassel, author of *Working Ourselves to Death*, was recently interviewed by the *San Francisco Chronicle*. She said,

> A group of insurance agencies asked me to investigate a trend they couldn't understand. They were getting a surprisingly high number of claims for 30-day in-patient drug and alcohol treatment of children of employees. I found that the parents of these kids were workaholics—their life was unmanageable, they were obsessed with business and deadlines and success. Their kids were in quite a bit of emotional pain from the lack of connection they felt toward their parents and had begun acting out with drugs and alcohol. The irony was that the kids were going to treatment while the parents, who were addicts, remained untreated. That was because in the adults, addiction wasn't seen as real; it appeared to be a normal way of life.

*Workaholics
are losers*
Fassel's book says that workaholism is socially promoted because it is seemingly socially productive; but the truth, according to her, is that workaholics end up costing companies money

because they produce in spurts. Rushaholic work addicts look busy, but they are usually moving so fast that they make mistakes.

Along with robbing you of time, abuse of work by overwork leads to stress, causes you and others to make mistakes, penalizes your customers with shoddy service, and therefore has a negative impact on quality. The guerrilla entrepreneur does not have a wealth of experience with six-day weeks, ten-hour days, weekends that are no different from weekdays, or canceled vacations.

That same guerrilla *does know* what it's like to work twenty days in a row, to burn gallons of midnight oil, and to sacrifice a holiday for a work emergency. But these are exceptions to the rule. And the rule reminds you that *you are a human being first and a worker second.*

My three-day workweek, a sweet joy of my guerrilla existence, has been a seven-day workweek several times, but since I've been working this way (for more than a quarter-century), I can count the seven-day workweeks on the fingers of my two hands. I've worked past midnight too, but again, fewer than ten times. And I've had to cancel a holiday at the last minute—once. My entrepreneurial life is consistently enriched with three- and four-week holidays, several each year, and my work output doesn't suffer—because I plan for all the free time, just as I plan my work time.

A sweet joy of guerrilla existence

Just as I rarely allow a play opportunity to erode my workday, I hardly ever allow a work opportunity to eat into my free time. I write this after spending ninety minutes late Saturday night making notes for an upcoming project and then entering them in my word processor on Sunday before the FortyNiners game. A guerrilla just has to be flexible. Even an orderly life is riddled with exceptions. As author Anne Lamott says in her wonderful book *Bird by Bird,* "I tell my plans to God and she laughs."

Who is in control of your destiny? *You are.* Once you understand the truth of that, you'll not veer down the road leading to

Who controls your destiny?

workaholism, you'll know how to keep stress further away than arm's length, and you'll eventually become consciously addicted to a life with balance.

This will not occur simply because you have free time from work, but because you'll know *what to do* with that free time. If you don't, you have no business planning to be a guerrilla entrepreneur in the first place. The guerrilla has an abundance of free-time pursuits and cannot recollect ever having been bored. That's because the guerrilla creates—or re-creates—her business so that workaholism and stress are not part of the plan. I write my weekly chores in my calendar on the days that say Monday, Tuesday, and Wednesday. If there are more tasks to be accomplished, I flip the calendar to the next Monday, Tuesday, and Wednesday. I rarely write a business task for a Thursday or a Friday, a Saturday or a Sunday.

If I'm scheduled to give a talk on a Friday, I do it. Do I, in return, plan to skip work on Monday, Tuesday, or Wednesday of that week? No. I love working on Mondays, Tuesdays, and Wednesdays, and I love the work I do, so I dive into it.

I used to work at one of the great advertising agencies on the planet, Leo Burnett, in Chicago. There, it was known that if you worked late or on weekends or brought work home—except in emergency situations, which our clients were taught to avoid— you were doing something wrong, something stupid. And it happened because you didn't plan your workday well or couldn't handle your job because you were in over your head. Leo didn't want his people's minds burning out with workaholism, just as I want no guerrillas to toil when they should be goofing off, as God probably intended. He even went as far as designating a day for rest.

What God probably intended

It seems to me we're entitled to one extra day of rest per thousand years of living in the world and surviving together, such as we do. Three thousand years of evolving therefore nets us three extra days of not working. Add them to the one granted by God, and you've got the four-day weekend and the three-day workweek.

Hard work is absolutely necessary to success at the outset of a business undertaking, and more hours will be required at first. But the patterns you set at the outset will remain work habits that are difficult to break, often impossible as clients and customers get used to your schedule. It's better to get them used to the reality of your hours and not to their grandparents' concept of work hours.

Whereas hard work will benefit your business, overly hard work—in the form of draconian hours and days—will prevent you from operating at your sharpest. The guerrilla sees clearly the line between working hard and working too hard. The guerrilla uses the technologies of the day—computers, fax machines, cellular phones—to save time without sacrificing quality or creating stress. If you experience stress, something is wrong and it must be diagnosed. Stress is a symptom of operational illness. Cure that illness with planning and commitment, and the stress will be alleviated.

The side effects of hard work

Stress due to overwork has horrid side effects:

* It causes substantial increases in substance abuse, stress-related health problems, and the phenomenon of latchkey children left to fend for themselves and kids who feel as bonded to the day-care workers as they do to Mom and Dad.
* Half of all marriages will end in divorce. This guerrilla entrepreneur recently celebrated his fortieth wedding anniversary.
* Over 60 percent of all kids born today will spend some time growing up in a single-parent family.
* The incidence of reported child abuse has quadrupled in the last decade, and spousal abuse is rising at an ugly rate.
* The average age of successful suicides is now forty. And there has been a 300 percent increase in the suicide rate for fifteen- to twenty-four-year-olds since the middle of the century, probably connected to single parenting.
* Cocaine and alcohol abuse actively touches six out of ten American families.

* The average working parent spends a mere *eleven minutes a day* of "quality time" with his or her children.

In the study that reported these findings, conducted among working men, 74 percent of them said, "If I had to do it over again, I would spend more time with my family." A guerrilla entrepreneur would never say that because he has already arranged for free time at the very outset of his business existence.

Alas, many entrepreneurs who could be guerrillas and own themselves, instead of selling themselves into entrepreneurial slavery by working too much, allow their lives to be dictated by their *egos*. Their mindset tells them this: "If I don't do it, it won't be done right." Their mindset should stress this instead: "If I delegate this to the right person and train that person to do it right, it will get done right, and I'll still have the time to do other things." A head honcho at General Electric once said that you should make a list of the twenty things you are doing that make you a workaholic, and ten of them will be nonsense that you can dispense with. Of the other ten, how many do you suppose you can delegate?

Set finish times in advance

Guerrilla entrepreneurs ward off workaholism by setting their projected finish times in advance, since people will work to fill up the allotted time. They set reasonable deadlines for themselves and make sure their customers or clients do the same. They prioritize their work, eliminating the nonsense. They are so aware of time that they don't ever waste it, but always spend it wisely. They are keenly aware that work creates ruts and that their mission is to accomplish the work while preventing ruts from being formed, ruts than will trap them for the better part of a lifetime.

In the 1980s, working late was considered heroic and proper, a sign that the person was on her way to success. Work experts now inform us that this attitude has shifted, that there has been a dramatic change in perception, that mainstream thinking now holds that there is more to life than work. Says one time-management specialist: "I think the people who reject long hours will be the real leaders in the years to come—they're the brightest, the innovators. The guys logging really long hours aren't seen as heroes anymore. They're seen as turkeys."

When a person opts for workaholism, that person sacrifices his own humanity, willingly, for the almighty dollar. Or for status. Or power. Or because the workaholic is programmed like the worker ant—to toil without thinking, to set aside all sense of individuality. *The great sacrifice*

The guerrilla entrepreneur is very different from that fellow; the guerrilla is programmed to fulfill herself as a human being, to assert her individuality and nourish it, to encourage it to bloom. We just didn't have the time for such reflection in the nine-to-five atmosphere of this past century. Our parents and grandparents set a pace that was ideal for them, but wrong for us—living as we do in an age brimming with leisure pursuits and the spiritual enlightenment to realize their importance.

This age brings both good news and bad news. The good news is that along with the new millennium, we are entering a new world of work, in which time and technology will take on new perspectives, in which people will actually take time to reflect upon their existence and work style. *Good news and bad news*

The bad news is that not everyone is going to enter that new world. Some will be impeded by old notions and false perceptions. A lead article in *The National Geographic*, which reported on the impact of information on the world, concluded with these words:

> Some of us will cross into the new world; others will remain behind. New worlders will pull even further ahead as technologies evolve. . . . Technology promises more and more information for less and less effort. As we hear these promises, we must balance faith in technology with faith in ourselves. Wisdom and insight often come not from keeping up-to-date or compiling facts but from quiet reflection. What we hold most valuable—things like morality and compassion—can be found only within us. While embrac-

ing the future, we can remain loyal to our unchanging humanity.

Workaholism, burnout, and stress were bugaboos of the bad old days. The guerrilla lives in the present and wants it to be primarily made up of the good new days, so he makes the most of every precious moment and does not mortgage the present for the future.

32

Ten Pitfalls to Avoid in Your Quest

YOU SHOULD KNOW that there are more than ten pitfalls awaiting you on your journey to guerrilla entrepreneurship. Ten thousand is more like it. To avoid most of them, keep your mental eyes open, and visualize the best while remembering that the worst is visualizing you. Guerrilla entrepreneurs are well acquainted with Murphy and his laws, consider him a wild-eyed optimist, and have learned to cross the street when they see him coming. You can avoid him too—merely by side-stepping the ten tempting entrepreneur traps. Wise men and women have been lured into them, never to escape.

A guerrilla entrepreneur once said that she didn't want to be a passenger in her own life. That meant she had to assume the captaincy of her future and be in complete charge of all attainments and goof-offs, even fatal goof-offs. She had to learn to fend off temptation daily. Many entrepreneurs are lured by "opportunities"—siren calls urging them to stray from their goals and wander off into someone else's dream. Guerrillas remain firmly committed to their own dreams.

All ten pitfalls listed here are traps you've probably foreseen anyway. The more you recognize them at the outset, the less likely you'll be to tumble into them when they're on your path. So take a few moments to peer down into them. The next time you see them, you can smile as you leap over them.

Pitfall #1: The Time Trap

As much as people revere leisure time, they have less of it than ever, averaging 32 percent less leisure time than they had in the

32% less leisure time

1980s. Here I am jumping up and glorifying the three-day work-week while increasing numbers of Americans are wondering how to get out from under the six-day workweek. Becoming a guerrilla entrepreneur is the best way I know. But avoid doing all the work yourself, letting your ego get in the way of your dreams, failing to make the distinction between spending time and wasting time. If you find yourself spending too much time at the outset, you'll establish a pattern that will be very difficult to change later on. Habits are much easier to form than they are to break. "I'll just work sixty hours a week for now, and then I'll cut back later." It won't happen.

Pitfall #2: The Large Lure

While working my three-day workweek and pulling in acceptable dollars, I used to wonder, but not very often, how much money I could make if I worked a six-day week. But the thought of giving up my four-day weekend was always too horrendous, and I lost little time entertaining that grandiose, stupid thought. More than a few times, clients have offered me alluring opportunities to do more for them for more money—which would have resulted in putting in more time. I accepted each opportunity, but with my proviso that I maintain the integrity of my work schedule. You'll be offered chances to earn more money, expand, take on more people, move to a larger space, and transform your business from an entrepreneurial endeavor to a large corporate entity. Hey, it's your life—but you've got to turn in your guerrilla credentials if you opt for size rather than freedom, for bigness rather than balance.

Pitfall #3: The Money Morass

Said *Fortune* magazine, "Those driven solely by the desire for big bucks tend to be negligent of personal relationships. The lack of time away from work for falling in love, sitting and talking with a spouse, or answering a child's question" contributes to the fact that mental health providers constitute a major growth industry. Money alters human behavior to the point that it causes well-meaning owners of small businesses, bound for success, to veer in the direction of financial success, steam-rolling their chances for emotional, marital, parental, or social success. Money, which is easier to attain than balance is, is more frequently sought. Those who pursue it find that the price they pay outstrips the money they gain. Anyhow, how do you put a price tag on a happy marriage or a well-adjusted kid? Of all the pitfalls, the Money Morass is the deepest, darkest, and biggest. If you fall into it, don't expect to find any fellow guerrillas at the bottom with you. They've learned that it is possible to earn a living without paying for it with their lives. *The deepest pit of all*

Pitfall #4: The Burnout Barrier

You'll search your soul to come up with a method for earning your livelihood, and you'll set up shop with all the right intentions. You'll work hard and smart, and your effort will bear fruit. But somewhere along the way, you might lose some of your initial enthusiasm for your work. You'll continue on because you've been successful, but you'll bring less and less joy to your work. The thrill will be gone. You'll have burned out.

If this happens to you, aim to *do something else.* You must make a change, large or small, to restore your enthusiasm—for without it, you're sunk. The trouble is, most business owners continue on without joy, not wanting to rock the boat that got them to their destination—even though that destination now means being lost at sea. They are bogged down by habit, by routine. If the spark is gone, get yourself another dream. Enthusiasm will fuel your fires, and if it is absent, the fire in your soul will go out—the fire that was the key to your success. Guerrillas know that they can relight the fire for a new venture, and studies irrevocably prove that the more you love what you do, the better you'll do it. So if you no longer feel the love, end the relationship and start another.

Pitfall #5: The Humanity Hindrance

I know I'm urging you to become an efficient earning machine, to realize the crucial importance of profits to a business, to work from home if you can, and to embrace technology as a means to your end. But I hope like crazy that you never lose your personal warmth, your sense of humor, or your love of other human beings in your quest to become a successful entrepreneur. Sadly, the world has more than enough tales of individuals who left a trail of shattered people on their climb to the top. The guerrilla's priority list places people ahead of business, family ahead of business, love ahead of business, self ahead of business. Keeping your eyes on the bottom line should not make them beady. Putting your heart in your work should not turn it to stone. Attaining everything on your wish list should not put you on anybody's enemy list. An executive I knew at a Fortune 500 company had a glass eye. When I asked which was the glass eye, I was told, "It's the warm one." No rule says that you must give up your humanity as the dues for achieving entrepreneurial success.

*The guerrilla's
priority list*

Pitfall #6: The Focus Foil

Along the road to your goals you'll find many sparkling roadside attractions beckoning you to stop for a while to linger. Linger you should, for investigation is the hallmark of the guerrilla. But be certain to maintain focus on your goals while you're checking out the scenery. It is not difficult to lose that focus and aim for a false goal, a tangential journey leading away from your dreams. You can become so involved in the details of your operation that you deviate from your primary thrust. Your time will become gobbled up by details instead of broad strokes. You can become wrapped up in a technology such as computer games, losing your focus. You spend your time learning about your computer instead of broadening your business. Grow your mind as you grow your business, but maintain your direction — unless you consciously decide to make a change. I have nothing against a wholesale change, but if it is made by circumstances instead of by you, it's a major problem. Don't let your focus be foiled by anything except your own conscious intent.

*Growing
your mind*

Pitfall #7: The Perfection Pit

At the top of my own list of time-wasters, life-stealers, and company-ruiners are perfectionists and the pursuit of perfection. I am all for excellence and admire perfection in a bowling game or classroom attendance—two areas where perfection is possible. But how many drafts of a manuscript must a writer make? Does it become a perfect manuscript after the twentieth rewrite? I doubt it. Many entrepreneurs become ensnared by their own high standards and the quest for elusive perfection. I am giddy with delight that the pilot who commands the jet carrying me to God-knows-where is a perfectionist. Same for the people who made the plane. And when I watch my wife skydive, I can only pray her parachute was packed by a perfectionist. But I don't recommend perfection as a goal—unless public safety is at risk. Instead, I recommend it as a guide. Guerrillas try to be perfect but don't spend all their time and energy attaining it. They know that the world is teeming with entrepreneurs who spend half their time polishing the unpolishable, steeped in the unnecessary, devoted to the unattainable. A perfect memo? A perfect direct mail letter? A perfect design scheme? Give me a break. May your enterprise be free from imperfections and from perfectionists.

Free from imperfections and perfectionists

Pitfall #8: The Selling Snare

The selling snare forces you to sell the same thing over and over again. The guerrilla's way around it is to *make multiple sales with one effort.* Instead of a single issue of a magazine, sell a subscription. Rather than a single massage, sell a year's worth of weekly massages. Guerrillas do all in their power to develop products or services that must be purchased on a regular basis. You work hard to close a sale. If you've got to get up and do it again and again, the bloom may soon fade from your entrepreneurial rose. But if you work just as hard and manage to close ten years' worth of sales, that bloom will enjoy a long period of radiance. Many offerings are sold with repeat sales built right in, from my own *Guerrilla Marketing Newsletter* to cable television, from cleaning services to diaper services, from insurance coverage to gardening, from swimming pool maintenance to dental care. Apply the ultimate in selling skills so that your one-time sale can lead to years and years of profits. If you fall into the trap of selling single shots only, you'll be spending more time selling than enjoying the benefits of your efforts.

Pitfall #9: The Leisure Lure

Don't kid yourself into believing that leisure time is automatically a good thing. Leisure time, when you don't know what do to with it, can lead to a wide variety of problems—from boredom to substance abuse. Truth be told, many people actually enjoy their work time more than their leisure time because at least they know what they'll be doing with their work time—they haven't a clue about how to spend their leisure hours. Guerrillas do have a clue. And a hobby. And a slew of interests beyond working and earning money. They enjoy their leisure almost as much as their work because they are working at something they love and because they've given a lot of thought to what they'll do with their free time. They know that free time by itself can be a drag.

Free time can be a drag

What do I do with all my free time? I ski, go river rafting, hike, play golf, explore by car, camp in the wilderness, watch TV, talk with my wife, play poker, travel, fish, canoe, hang-glide, play tennis, toss the Frisbee, shoot baskets, go bird watching, go to ballgames, investigate San Francisco, check out tide pools, stare at waves, write poetry, soak in a hot tub, walk a mile each day, socialize in online chat rooms, visit museums, go to the zoo, read voraciously, roll on the floor with my pussycats, explore cyberspace, take my pup to the beach, and climb rocks. I have zero problems with free time and can always fill it. And occasionally I take immense pleasure at going to sleep knowing I have accomplished absolutely nothing that day. Goofing off is one of my leisure activities. Instead of a vice, in this competitive and entrepreneurial age, it's a guerrilla virtue.

Pitfall #10: The Retirement Ruse

Horrid but true: more than 75 percent of retirees die within two years of their retirement. When they retire from work, it's as though they also retire from life. Don't make the mistake of planning for retirement. Plan on cutting down, on easing off, but not on quitting altogether.

My three-day workweek will probably shrink to a two-day workweek when I'm seventy-five years old, though it depresses me to give up that day of writing. Maybe I'll rethink that plan when I'm older and wiser. Working keeps you sharp, keeps your brain in shape. Ceasing to work allows your brain to atrophy. What are most retirees concerned with? Well, 38 percent say they don't have enough money. Another 29 percent say they're fearful of not staying healthy. Eight percent say they have too much time on their hands, and they're bored. And 8 percent figure they probably won't live long enough to enjoy life.

Guerrillas have enough money because they put retirement into the same category as imprisonment. The money continues to flow into their lives long after their cohorts have retired. They stay healthy because continuing to hone the edge caused by work results in the maintenance of health and increased longevity. They do not suffer from the problem of having too much time, because they have just enough for work, just enough for play. And they have been enjoying life all along because they've been engaged in the work they love, a trademark of the guerrilla entrepreneur. In nature, nothing ever retires, and as we get closer to understanding our own relationship with nature, we are discovering that retirement is unhealthy and contraindicated in anyone with brain waves.

It's okay to retire from work, just as long as you remain active in something else. Golf is okay. So is mastering the Internet. Walking in the woods qualifies as a worthwhile activity. And so do painting and photography. As an entrepreneur, you are your own boss. No one is going to *make* you retire. If you are no longer interested in the work your business provides you, find a different job for yourself within your own company. That's the luxury of being your own boss, calling your own shots. But what happens if you are simply no longer interested in the business? My advice is to retire from it—then move on to another dream. If perfecting your golf game is your next dream, go for it. But just

Planning for retirement is like planning for suicide

don't retire from life itself. The trap of planning for retirement is like planning your own slow suicide—brought on by inactivity.

The guerrilla entrepreneur knows the ten pitfalls very well, possibly even knows people who have fallen into them or who are heading toward them. By being familiar with the enemy, the guerrilla proceeds unimpeded, gracefully avoiding the temptations that beckon to all entrepreneurs.

33

The Need for Passion

WHAT'S MORE IMPORTANT to the success of a business than common sense, experience, and enlightenment? I'll bet you answered the question correctly with your first guess—if your first guess was *passion*. If you lack it, the work style of the guerrilla entrepreneur probably is not for you.

Lack of passion is often the real, though not the obvious, reason for business failure. Famed philosopher Joseph Campbell wasn't addressing entrepreneurs, but could have been, when he said, "Follow your bliss." Where bliss exists, passion probably flourishes as well. No bliss most likely means no passion. Sadly, many businesses are started by people who have the passion and have the bliss. When both fade, which sometimes happens, the businesses continue; but they have lost their original fervor and momentum, and the result is usually depressing, both emotionally and financially.

"Follow your bliss"

That's why the true guerrilla constantly assesses herself to ensure that the passion is indeed present. Ideally, it burns with increased vigor as time passes. My own passion for my work has increased every year since I started, and I can forecast no diminishment in the future, only increased enthusiasm as I continue to see the results of the work.

Is there a difference between interest and passion? Yes, and it's exactly the same as the difference between *like* and *love*. Passion involves intensity. It comes from deep within you. It is all-consuming. It burns. There are ten areas in which guerrillas feel honest passion—not obsession or compulsion, but sincere

Liking and loving

passion. Reach down into yourself to measure your own passion about these aspects of your life:

1. *You feel passion toward your product or service.* If you don't feel it, it will be difficult to muster the enthusiasm that fuels consistent sales. Enthusiasm, like passion itself, is contagious. If you have it, your staff and suppliers, your customers and network members feel it as well. If you don't, your apathy will spread to those same people.

2. *You feel passion toward your customers.* You want them to get exactly what they need. Your understanding of them ensures that their needs and your offerings are an ideal match. You feel passionate about your ability to satisfy your customers. If you don't, they're going to sense it, and someone else's passion will woo them from you.

3. *You feel passion about your company.* You know how hard you work to do things right and to connect with people who will treat your customers like royalty. You have a vision for your company, and you know how to turn it into a glorious reality. Your passion keeps you focused on this vision and guides your behavior in running your business. Like basketball fans who say "I love this game!" in commercials, you frequently find yourself thinking, "I love this company!" If you aren't able to sincerely think that thought, make changes so that you can.

I love this company!

4. *You feel passion about your employees or network members.* As a guerrilla, you hired or joined forces with these people because of their attitude, and you feel good chemistry in relation to them. You know how hard they've worked for you, how they give your goals such high priority, how valuable they are to you. No wonder you feel such passion. They return it by their commitment to your company and by being passionate themselves.

5. *You feel passion about your day-to-day work.* Don't just sit there and take such a bold statement for granted. A lot of people are doing work for which they felt passion once upon a time, but no longer. If that's you, get yourself another line of work— please. You don't want to hold back your company or fellow networkers because you no longer feel the thrill you once felt. Do something different for the company, or do entirely different

work yourself. After all, we're talking about your life, and that gets top priority in the passion department.

6. *You feel passion about your marketing.* If you don't, be sure that someone in your company does. Ideally, you will feel strongly about it even if you're not the person creating it. After all, marketing does supply the power that makes your company grow, that produces profits, that keeps the morale up. If you do not feel passion about creating your marketing, I hope you feel it for the marketing itself and especially for the results it brings about for your firm.

7. *You feel passion about your service.* You don't confine service to what's written in a policy, but instead know that great service is whatever the customer wants it to be. You are passionate about giving that kind of service. After all, that's the kind of service you'd love to receive yourself. If you feel passion about rendering superlative service, your customers sense it and remember it. If you don't feel passion, they also sense it and remember it.

8. *You feel passion about improving.* You are not content to kick back and congratulate yourself on work well done. Instead, you know that smart people are constantly trying to make your customers their customers, so you feel passion about being the best company in your community or industry, or both. As long as your quality and service are of superb quality, you are not afraid of change, only of falling behind. Your passion for improvement keeps you the best.

How to be the best

9. *You feel passion about learning.* You know the importance of knowledge in the coming millennium and that the most powerful basic human instinct is to learn. As a guerrilla, you feel passionate about becoming better informed, smarter, and more knowledgeable about everything connected with your company, as well as your life. The day you stop feeling passion about learning is the day you may be on the way to becoming illiterate. Alvin Toffler, the author of *Future Shock*, said, "The illiterate of the future will not be the person who cannot read. It will be the person who does not know how to learn." And famed UCLA basketball coach John Wooden added, "It's what you learn after

you know it all that counts." Will you ever reach a point when you think you know it all?

10. *You feel passion about being a guerrilla entrepreneur.* That passion carries with it a devotion to a life of balance. It means you feel passionate about freedom and time, arranging your life so that you have enough of those precious gifts built into it to enjoy the fruits of your business. You are an entrepreneur bound for success and enjoying the journey, but you are a human being first, who values more in life than financial gain and increased size.

The guerrilla's edge

Fortunately, as a guerrilla, you've got an edge. This edge keeps the fires of your *passion* burning brightly. It gives you a decided advantage over the entrepreneurs who preceded you because it helps you avoid their mistakes and build upon their successes. It is, without question, the way of the guerrilla.

You've got the guerrilla's edge in *insight*. You've given thought to your priorities. You aren't going to be misled by the entrepreneurial myths involving overwork, overgrowth, and overextending your reach. You realize that your journey is your destination and that your plan is your road map. This insight will help you maintain your passion.

You've got the guerrilla's edge in *relationships*. Every sale you make leads to a lasting relationship. Every customer you get is going to be a customer for life. Your sales and even your profits will probably go up and down, but your number of relationships will constantly go up, and your sales and profits will eventually follow.

You've got the guerrilla's edge in *service*. You see your service from your customer's point of view, not merely from your own. You realize that your service gives you an enormous competitive advantage over those who may be larger but less devoted to making and keeping customers delighted with your company. You know well the power of word-of-mouth marketing and how it derives from excellent service.

You've got the guerrilla's edge in *flexibility*. You are not enslaved by company policies and by precedent. Instead, you are fast on your feet, sensitive to customer needs, and aware that flexibility is a tool for building relationships, profits, and your overall company. You are guided by the situation at hand and not by the way things were done in the past. Your flexibility adds to the passion that others feel about your company.

You've got the guerrilla's edge in *follow-up*. You don't have to be reminded about the number of potential relationships that are destroyed when customers are ignored after they make a purchase. Rather than ignore them, you pay attention to them, remind them of how glad you are that they're customers, and pepper them with special offers, inside information, and care. They never feel ignored by you and reciprocate by never ignoring your company when it comes to repeat purchases or referrals.

You have the guerrilla's edge in *cooperation*. You see other businesses as potential partners of yours, as firms that can help you as you help them. You don't keep your eye peeled for competitors to annihilate, but for businesses to team up with to form networks. Your attitude will help you prosper in an era when people are forming small businesses in droves.

You have the guerrilla's edge in *patience*. As a guerrilla, you are not in a hurry, never in a rush. You know how important time is, but you also know how too much speed results in diminished quality. Because of your planning, you avoid emergencies and high-pressure situations. Patience is one of your staunchest allies.

You have the guerrilla's edge in *economy*. You know how to market without investing a bundle of hard-earned money. You have learned that time and energy are valuable substitutes for large budgets. You realize that in most business activity, you have a choice of any two of these three factors: speed, economy, and quality. You always opt for economy and quality. Your patience helps you economize.

You have the guerrilla's edge in *timeliness*. You run a streamlined operation, devoid of fluff or unnecessary work. Your comfort with technology allows you to operate at maximum effectiveness. Your business is a state-of-the-art enterprise because it operates in the environment of today rather than that of ten years ago. Although you focus on your plan, you know the magic of proper timing and can make adjustments so that you are available just when customers need you.

You have the guerrilla's edge in *commitment*. This commitment will set you apart from many other businesses. It will help you achieve your aims with confidence. It is so powerful that you feel passion toward the commitment itself—enabling the passion to power your commitment, and the commitment to power your passion. Without this inner commitment, even the best plans may go awry. With it, plans turn into a bright reality.

The radiant light of love

The closer you examine it, the more you see that the way of the guerrilla is illuminated by the radiant light of *love*—love of self, work, family, others, freedom, independence, life. The guerrilla has a lifelong love affair with life. The deeper and more heartfelt her love, the more she is capable of generating the fiery and exquisite passion that fuels her business and ignites her entire life.

The time has never been better

In the history of humankind, there has never been a better time to be a guerrilla entrepreneur than right now. All the circumstances are now in your favor—the mindset, the technology, the splintering of many large businesses into even more small businesses.

Throughout the world, others are embarking on the same path that you will tread. Many are entrepreneurs, but few are guerrillas. Some will fail because they are playing by old rules in a new economy. Some will fail because the lure of largeness is too strong. Some will fail because they don't understand the role of balance in their lives.

But the guerrillas will succeed.

They will not judge the future by the past. They will be able to place work in the proper perspective. They will feel a sense of continual excitement about what they do. And they will be well aware of their edge over others.

Their passion—the fire in their hearts—will serve as the ultimate edge.

Acknowledgments

An author never has enough space to acknowledge all the people who made a book possible. So I won't even try. After all, you've been reading a lot and don't need my expressions of gratitude here at the end to detract from your guerrilla momentum. I remember Oscar winners who won my admiration for their work, then lost it completely with their TV acceptance speeches. If you're with me up till now, I sure don't want to lose you here.

My first acknowledgment is to my incredible wife, Patsy, who demonstrates the flexibility and understanding crucial in a guerrilla's mate. I thank my daughter, Amy, for her continuing inspiration in the way she lives her life. I publically thank for the zillionth time my agents, Michael Larsen and Elizabeth Pomada, for creating the environment in my head that motivated this book. As president of Guerrilla Marketing International, Bill Shear has made my life as smooth as he has made it delightful. Marnie Patterson, my editor, improved this book with every comment she made. Susanna Brougham is the one who made it readable. Joanne White did the grunt work. And finally, I thank Deborah Brockman for her feedback, insight, and empathy.

I am lucky to owe gratitude to such wonderful people.

**You can continue to be a guerrilla with
The Guerrilla Marketing Newsletter . . .**

Published continuously since 1986, *The Guerrilla Marketing Newsletter* provides you with up-to-the-minute insights to maximize the profits you can obtain through marketing. The newsletter is written to furnish you with the cream of the new guerrilla marketing information from around the world, along with new perspectives on existing wisdom about marketing. It is filled with practical advice, the latest research, upcoming trends, and brand-new marketing techniques—all designed to pay off in profits to you.

A yearly subscription costs $59 for six issues.

All subscribers are given this unique and powerful guarantee: if you aren't convinced after examining your first issue for thirty days that the newsletter will raise your profits, your subscription fee will be refunded — along with $2 just for trying.

To subscribe and get a free brochure, call, write, or e-mail us at

Guerrilla Marketing International
260 Cascade Drive, P.O. Box 1336
Mill Valley, CA 94902, U.S.A.
1-800-748-6444 (In California, 415-381-8361)
E-mail: GM INTL@aol.com

If you're online, check the Guerrilla Marketing Online Magazine at http://www.gmarketing.com.

Get the Complete Guerrilla Arsenal!

Guerrilla Marketing: Secrets for Making Big Profits from Your Small Business   ISBN 0-395-64496-8 $11.95

The book that started the Guerrilla Marketing revolution, now completely revised and updated for the nineties. Full of the latest strategies, information on the latest technologies, new programs for targeted prospects, and management lessons for the twenty-first century.

Guerrilla Financing: Alternative Techniques to Finance Any Small Business   ISBN 0-395-52264-1 $10.95

The ultimate sourcebook for finance in the 1990s, and the first book to describe in detail all the traditional and alternative sources of funding for small and medium-size businesses.

Guerrilla Marketing Attack: New Strategies, Tactics, and Weapons for Winning Big Profits   ISBN 0-395-50220-9 $9.95

A companion to *Guerrilla Marketing*, this book arms small and medium-size business with vital information about direct marketing, customer relations, cable TV, desktop publishing, ZIP code inserts, TV shopping networks, and much more.

Guerrilla Marketing Excellence: The Fifty Golden Rules for Small-Business Success   ISBN 0-395-60844-9 $9.95

Jay Levinson delivers the 50 basic truths of guerrilla marketing that can make or break your company, including the crucial difference between profits and sales, marketing in a recession, and the latest uses of video and television to assure distribution.

Guerrilla Selling: Unconventional Weapons and Tactics for Increasing Your Sales   ISBN 0-395-57820-5 $9.95

Today's increasingly competitive business environment requires new skills and commitment from salespeople. Guerrilla Selling presents unconventional selling tactics that are essential for success.

The Guerrilla Marketing Handbook
ISBN 0-395-70013-2 $14.95

The Guerrilla Marketing Handbook presents Jay Levinson's entire arsenal of marketing weaponry, including a step-by-step guide to developing a marketing campaign and detailed descriptions of over 100 marketing tools.

Guerrilla Advertising: Cost-Effective Tactics for
Small-Business Success   ISBN 0-395-68718-9 $11.95

Jay Levinson applies his proven guerrilla philosophy to advertising. Teeming with anecdotes about past and current advertising successes and failures, the book entertains as it teaches the nuts and bolts of advertising for small businesses.

Guerrilla Marketing Online
ISBN 0-395-72859-2 $12.95

From getting aquainted to Internet culture to creating a complete online marketing plan, *Guerilla Marketing Online* offers the basic training entrepreneurs need to take Jay Levinson's proven marketing tactics to the new and important marketplace of the Internet.

Guerrilla Marketing Online Weapons
ISBN 0-395-77019-X $12.95

One hundred online marketing strategies to help businesses take advantage of the Internet's great marketing potential. From e-mail addresses and signatures to storefronts, feedback mechanisms, electronic catalogs, and press kits, *Guerrilla Marketing Online Weapons* will help any business, small or large, define, refine, and put its message on the Net with ease.

These titles are available through bookstores, or you can order directly from Houghton Mifflin at 1-800-225-3362.

A BLUEPRINT FOR SUCCESS WITHOUT STRESS, NOW AND IN THE FUTURE

Jay Conrad Levinson best-selling author and guru of the guerrilla lifestyle, has now applied his proven guerrilla tactics to entrepreneurship in the twenty-first century. Covering everything from preparing a focused mission statement to hiring responsible employees and delegating effectively to sustaining a balanced and fulfilled personal life, *The Way of the Guerrilla* is an invaluable guide to the future for new and seasoned business owners alike.

JAY CONRAD LEVINSON, president of Guerrilla Marketing International, lectures around the world on guerrilla business techniques. He is the author or coauthor of twelve titles in the Guerrilla Marketing series. A happily married man who has lived the life of a balanced and successful entrepreneur for more than thirty years, he resides in northern California.